SUZAN-LORI PARKS

Theatre includes *Topdog/Underdog* (Pulitzer Prize), *Porgy and Bess* (Tony Award for Best Revival of a Musical), *The Book of Grace*, *Unchain My Heart: The Ray Charles Musical*, *In the Blood*, *The Death of the Last Black Man in the Whole Entire World aka the Negro Book Of The Dead*, *Venus*, *The America Play*, *Father Comes Home From The Wars (Parts 1, 2 and 3)* and *Fucking A*. Her project *365 Days/365 Plays* – where she wrote a play a day for an entire year – was produced in over seven hundred theatres worldwide, creating one of the largest grassroots collaborations in theatre history. Upcoming: *Plays for the Plague Year*.

Film and television includes *The United States vs Billie Holiday* (writer) and *Genius: Aretha* (showrunner/executive producer/head writer).

Her novel *Getting Mother's Body* is published by Random House.

Suzan-Lori is a MacArthur Fellow and was the first African-American woman to win a Pulitzer Prize for Drama.

In her spare time, she writes songs and fronts her band Sula & The Noise.

Other Titles in this Series

Annie Baker
THE ANTIPODES
THE FLICK
JOHN

Jez Butterworth
THE FERRYMAN
JERUSALEM
JEZ BUTTERWORTH PLAYS: ONE
JEZ BUTTERWORTH PLAYS: TWO
MOJO
THE NIGHT HERON
PARLOUR SONG
THE RIVER
THE WINTERLING

Tearrance Arvelle Chisholm
BR'ER COTTON

Caryl Churchill
BLUE HEART
CHURCHILL PLAYS: THREE
CHURCHILL PLAYS: FOUR
CHURCHILL PLAYS: FIVE
CHURCHILL: SHORTS
CLOUD NINE
DING DONG THE WICKED
A DREAM PLAY *after* Strindberg
DRUNK ENOUGH TO SAY I LOVE YOU?
ESCAPED ALONE
FAR AWAY
GLASS. KILL. BLUEBEARD'S FRIENDS.
    IMP.
HERE WE GO
HOTEL
ICECREAM
LIGHT SHINING IN BUCKINGHAMSHIRE
LOVE AND INFORMATION
MAD FOREST
A NUMBER
PIGS AND DOGS
SEVEN JEWISH CHILDREN
THE SKRIKER
THIS IS A CHAIR
THYESTES *after* Seneca
TRAPS
WHAT IF IF ONLY

Natasha Gordon
NINE NIGHT

debbie tucker green
BORN BAD
DEBBIE TUCKER GREEN PLAYS: ONE
DIRTY BUTTERFLY
EAR FOR EYE
HANG
NUT
A PROFOUNDLY AFFECTIONATE,
    PASSIONATE DEVOTION TO
    SOMEONE (– *NOUN*)
RANDOM
STONING MARY
TRADE & GENERATIONS
TRUTH AND RECONCILIATION

Jeremy O. Harris
SLAVE PLAY

Branden Jacobs-Jenkins
APPROPRIATE
GLORIA
AN OCTOROON

Arinzé Kene
GOD'S PROPERTY
GOOD DOG
LITTLE BABY JESUS & ESTATE WALLS
MISTY

Lucy Kirkwood
BEAUTY AND THE BEAST
    with Katie Mitchell
BLOODY WIMMIN
THE CHILDREN
CHIMERICA
HEDDA *after* Ibsen
IT FELT EMPTY WHEN THE HEART
    WENT AT FIRST BUT IT IS
    ALRIGHT NOW
LUCY KIRKWOOD PLAYS: ONE
MOSQUITOES
NSFW
TINDERBOX
THE WELKIN

Tony Kushner
ANGELS IN AMERICA –
    PARTS ONE AND TWO
CAROLINE, OR CHANGE
HOMEBODY/KABUL
THE VISIT, OR THE OLD LADY
    COMES TO CALL
    after Friedrich Dürrenmatt

Tracy Letts
AUGUST: OSAGE COUNTY
KILLER JOE

Bruce Norris
CLYBOURNE PARK
DOWNSTATE
THE LOW ROAD
THE PAIN AND THE ITCH
PURPLE HEART

Lynn Nottage
CRUMBS FROM THE TABLE OF JOY
INTIMATE APPAREL
RUINED
SWEAT

Chinonyerem Odimba
AMONGST THE REEDS
BLACK LOVE
PRINCESS & THE HUSTLER
UNKNOWN RIVERS

Janice Okoh
EGUSI SOUP
THE GIFT
THREE BIRDS

Suzan-Lori Parks
FATHER COMES HOME FROM THE
    WARS (PARTS 1, 2 & 3)
RED LETTER PLAYS
TOPDOG/UNDERDOG

Winsome Pinnock
LEAVE TAKING
ROCKETS AND BLUE LIGHTS
TAKEN
TITUBA

Eugene O'Neill
AH! WILDERNESS
ANNA CHRISTIE
    & THE EMPEROR JONES
DESIRE UNDER THE ELMS
    & GREAT GOD BROWN
THE HAIRY APE & ALL GOD'S
    CHILLUN GOT WINGS
THE ICEMAN COMETH
LONG DAY'S JOURNEY INTO NIGHT
MOURNING BECOMES ELECTRA
A MOON FOR THE MISBEGOTTEN
STRANGE INTERLUDE
A TOUCH OF THE POET

Suzan-Lori Parks

WHITE NOISE

NICK HERN BOOKS
London
www.nickhernbooks.co.uk

A Nick Hern Book

White Noise first published in Great Britain as a paperback original in 2021 by Nick Hern Books Limited, The Glasshouse, 49a Goldhawk Road, London W12 8QP, by special arrangement with Theatre Communications Group, Inc., New York

White Noise copyright © 2016–2021 Suzan-Lori Parks

Suzan-Lori Parks has asserted her right to be identified as the author of this work

Cover image: photography by Seamus Ryan; creative design by MUSE

Designed and typeset by Nick Hern Books, London
Printed in Great Britain by Mimeo Ltd, Huntingdon, Cambridgeshire PE29 6XX

A CIP catalogue record for this book is available from the British Library

ISBN 978 1 83904 050 4

CAUTION   All rights whatsoever in this play are strictly reserved. Requests to reproduce the text in whole or in part should be addressed to the publisher.

Performing Rights   Applications for performance, including readings and excerpts, by amateurs and professionals should be addressed to Olivier Sultan, CAA, 405 Lexington Avenue, 19th Floor, New York, NY 10174, *email* olivier.sultan@caa.com, *tel* (212) 277.9000

No performance of any kind may be given unless a licence has been obtained. Applications should be made before rehearsals begin. Publication of this play does not necessarily indicate its availability for performance.

*'Not everything can be changed.
But nothing can be changed until it is faced.'*

James Baldwin

White Noise was first performed at The Public Theater,
New York City, New York, on 20 March 2019. The cast was
as follows:

LEO	Daveed Diggs
DAWN	Zoe Winters
MISHA	Sheria Irving
RALPH	Thomas Sadoski
Director	Oskar Eustis
Set Designer	Clint Ramos
Costume Designer	Toni-Leslie James
Lighting Designer	Xavier Pierce
Sound Designer	Dan Moses Schreier
Projections	Lucy Mackinnon
Production Stage Manager	Buzz Cohen

The play received its European premiere at the Bridge Theatre,
London, on 12 October 2021 (previews from 5 October).
The cast was as follows:

LEO	Ken Nwosu
DAWN	Helena Wilson
MISHA	Faith Omole
RALPH	James Corrigan
Director	Polly Findlay
Set Designer	Lizzie Clachan
Costume Designer	Natalie Pryce
Movement Director	Jade Hackett
Lighting Designer	Jackie Shemesh
Sound Designer	Donato Wharton
Intimacy Coordinator	David Thackeray
Musical Director	Marc Tritschler
Assistant Director	John Rwothomack
Props Supervisor	Lily Mollgaard
Casting Director	Amy Ball
Production Manager	Marty Moore
Costume Supervisor	Zoe Hammond
Creative Consultant	Mandy Hackett
Dramaturg	Jesse Cameron Alick

From the Author's Elements of Style

I'm continuing the use of my slightly unconventional theatrical elements. Here's a road map.

(*Rest*.)
Take a little time, a pause, a breather; make a transition.

A Spell
An elongated and heightened (*Rest*.)
Denoted by repetition of figures' names with no dialogue.
Has sort of an architectural look:

LEO
DAWN
LEO
DAWN

This is a place where the figures experience their pure true state. While no action or stage business is necessary, directors should fill this moment as they best see fit.

[Brackets in the text indicate optional cuts for production.]

/Forward slashes indicate overlapping spoken text/

Characters

LEO, *early thirties, of African descent*
DAWN, *early thirties, of European descent*
MISHA, *early thirties, of African descent*
RALPH, *early thirties, of European descent*

The action takes place in a thriving city.

This text went to press before the end of rehearsals and so may differ slightly from the play as performed.

ACT ONE

Scene One: Leo's Solo

LEO. I can't sleep. All right? It's been going on for quite some time. When I was a baby, you know, born in the city, born directly into the urban environment, I would sleep. Like a rock. When I was one, or 2, or 3, I might get up to ask for some water, I was wearing a diaper so I wouldn't be getting up to pee, but sometimes I'd get up when I'd hear Mom and Pops, doing it, you know, making those love-sounds they'd make, but when I was a kid, up until I was 5 years old, every night when I hit the pillow, I would be *out*. My friends, all of us growing up in the same hood, all of us looking the same, all of us having pretty much the same economic circumstance: One parental figure, or two, working hard or, you know, working hard looking for work. We were urban but none of us were <u>extreme</u> urban, none of us were 24/7 homeless, none of us had an obvious or debilitating parental drug situation or a problematic violent domestic-abuse situation that we had to get out from underneath. Our parents were just, parents, our apartments, were all about the same size and all the same shit going down on the streets around bedtime. Nobody I knew had it different from me. And, until the age of 5 years old, as far as I knew, all of us in my family, that being me and my mom and my dad, and then, everybody in school I knew, all of us were sleeping soundly through the night.

(*Rest.*)

And then, it was on the anniversary of MLK's assassination, I don't know which one, but whatever year it was, I was 5, and we were at a church service and afterwards there was a gathering in the church basement. And Ms Malvina, she was a church lady, and she was also a schoolteacher, she taught science, and also, she also, well, she enjoyed her flask.

And sometimes, she would be smelling like – like she had been enjoying her flask. And that day in the church basement, Ms Malvina, she took me gently by the shoulder and said 'Leo, I know you know how the sun shines up above. But do you also know that, one day, the sun is going to die? You know that, don't you? One day the sun is going to die, and everything in the whole world is gonna go all black.'
(*Rest.*)
She said this to me. In the church basement. I was 5. And from that day forward, I would wake up in the middle of the night. For the first year or so, I'd wake up and ask Mom and Pops if the sun was still shining. And when they told me it was, I didn't believe them, so I'd stay awake until sunrise. Night after night after night. Meanwhile, in school, I was doing all right. Sheer force of will. But Mom and Pops were worried. I went from being a black kid to being a black kid with anxiety. And while most black folks don't do therapy, my folks sent me so I went. Talk Therapy didn't work. So they took me to the doctor. The doctor didn't give me pills cause I was just a kid but, they did give me a diagnosis: *pediatric insomnia* and when I got older, old enough to take pills, I received the appropriate prescriptions in the appropriate dosages and I took the pills but they didn't work. They kept upping the dosages. Still no luck. If I'd of taken any more pills I could have fallen asleep forever and didn't nobody want that. So, in addition to my anxiety and, as a kind of sidecar to my insomnia, I developed a mistrust of medications. And I began to see a terrifying connection: Medication is linked inextricably to the Pharmaceutical Industrial Complex which is linked, of course, to the Prison Industrial Complex which is linked of course, part and parcel, to all the other crazy shit. *We will ensnare you in our system for our profit and your downfall.* I would have taken more pills if they'd of worked, but they didn't so I stopped. Nothing worked. They tried hypnosis. Herbal remedies. They checked me, more than once, to see if I had a brain tumor, then to see if I was a schizophrenic. They took me to those sleep centers. I was still pretty much fully functioning. Cause I had developed the habit of catnapping. At different

times throughout the day. I guess. I mean, I guess that's how
I maintained. And, of course, sheer force of will. Pediatric
insomnia had become adolescent insomnia. I graduated high
school. I had good grades and I had a sport. Shooting, if you
can believe it. Cause my pops was retired military and he had
started taking me to the gun range, thinking it'd relieve my
stress. It didn't, but I was good at it, so him and me kept it up.
And there was an opportunity in college where I could join the
gun club so I joined. Yeah, I went to college. And I graduated.
Just like in high school I had good grades and a sport.
Shooting again. My college was a small <u>liberal arts school</u>
with a <u>rifle team</u>. Go figure. But it was really something. And
me and my roommate, Ralph, his dad owned a gun range.
We were both lettermen on the team and, for four years in a
row, we led the team in a total and complete domination of the
sport. Me and Ralph, we were totally 'All American.' We were
'The Riflemen.' Both of us, we were courted by the Olympics.
Neither of us made the team, though. Ralph was too busy,
always 'otherwise engaged' and I had discovered art. Or – art
had discovered me – and I'd started painting.
(*Rest.*)
Me and Dawn and Misha and Ralph. We all went to the same
school. We all graduated. Misha was summa. Dawn was
almost summa. I was on the Dean's list, with a major in Art.
Studio Art. Ralph just barely scraped by but he graduated.
And I was dating Misha and Ralph was dating Dawn. And
we were all really happy.
(*Rest.*)
Back then, we even had a band. The four of us. We played
pop-rock. We called ourselves Clover. We had this song that
we all wrote together: 'All I want. All I want, now,' it got
some traction on the college radio and we would play it at
every gig we got. It was our happy place. But the music
faded – you've been there, you know how that goes. And
then Graduation! And we all went our separate ways.
I worked on my art. And I still had my insomnia. It was just
plain insomnia now. Nothing special about it really. I slept
less than other people I knew. That's all it was that's all it is.
And I worked harder. Still do. And the shortage of sleep has

made me, you could say, edgier, than most people. The work I make is fractured. And angry. And so, I'm the fractured and angry and edgy black visual artist. Or, was.
(*Rest.*)
A couple of years passed and, after a while, we were all living in the city again. Not the city where I grew up. A bigger city. Better. We reconfigured in different ways: Ralph fell in love with Misha and I fell in love with Dawn. I was doing well for myself. But the years of sleeplessness were wearing me down. At night, I would lie down in bed, next to Dawn, and I'd think 'I'm cured.' Until I realized that I was only pretending to sleep.
(*Rest.*)
And Ralph, he had this great idea.
(*Rest.*)
For my birthday, Ralph, my right-hand bro, he got me this white-noise machine.
(*Rest.*)
It was perfect. Just plug it in and it makes 'white noise.' *SSSSSSSSS*. You know the sound. It's the sound of the sea. The sound of static. Not silence, but the sound of silence. And I plugged it in and I got in bed and I listened to it and it worked. It was fucking magic. Why hadn't anyone thought of it before? I slept regular hours. Miraculous. The only problem was, I would go to paint in my studio and there was that sound still in my head. *SSSSSSSSS*. And all I did was listen to that sound. I couldn't hear or see or think of anything else. I couldn't make art. Not like that hasn't happened before, right, I'm an artist, right, I stare at the walls a lot. But finally, you know, that white-noise machine? I threw it away. And, yeah, my insomnia came roaring back, even though so far, to this day, my art-making still hasn't come back yet. But it will. I just gotta clear my head. It's not a big thing. Only, yeah, when my gallery would call me, to check in, I would yell at them and then I would duck their calls and then duck events where there was a chance I might run into them. I'd pretty much stay home altogether. Unable to sleep. My career had been taking off. And then it wasn't. And then I quit my gallery. Or they dropped me. Me and

Dawn, we're still good, but my reputation isn't strong enough for me to get another gallery and so I tell everybody, Dawn and Misha and Ralph and my mom, cause, you know, my pops is passed, I tell everybody that I quit my gallery over creative differences and my mom believes me, but of course Dawn and then Misha and Ralph, they all see right through it, so I tell them that I'm planning on taking a departure and that I'll be doing self-portraits. Self-portraits, yeah. Which, you know, I haven't exactly started yet.
(*Rest.*)
Because I can only hear that sound in my head. That sound of static. That sound of the sea. That sound, not of silence, but that sound of the sound of silence. I've got that in my head all the time loud and clear. I used to have nothing in my head, when I couldn't sleep I had nothing in my head and now, I can't sleep <u>and</u> I have that sound. The sound of that White-Noise machine. Even though I threw the machine away. And I can't sleep. And I can't think either. I've got a short fuse. Maybe I don't got no fuse at all. Anxiety. But I'm managing it all right. Catnaps. And sheer force of will. Cause when I can't sleep, I walk. At night. Around the block. I walk around and around. Just walking. And that's pretty much how this whole thing got started.

Scene Two: Dawn & Leo

Morning. A nice enough apartment in a nice enough part of town. Sound of a shower going. DAWN, *still in her sweatpants/ pajamas, exits the bathroom. She turns up the audio of her phone – turns it up loud.*

She's dancing, trying to shake off the explosive and heavy situation by dancing to that fun song their band made back in the day: 'Your Love to Love Me' (song ©SLP, 2016). To listen, here's the link: https://soundcloud.app.goo.gl/1XRfDjCToCM8anfB8

LEO, *offstage, in the bathroom, taking a shower.*

DAWN (*talking to* LEO). Listen up, babe! Let it take you to the happy place. Yes, it's a fucked-up world, but we're in it and not of it! We use shit for fuel!! You hear me, Leo? Babe? We are going to the good place and we're not going to let them win. Listen to the music and let it move you, right? It's moving me. I feel better already.
(*Singing along.*)
ALL I WANT.
ALL I WANT, NOW. ALL I WANT.
I JUST WANT YOUR LOVE TO LOVE ME.

LEO (*from the shower*). I can't really hear you, hon.

DAWN *peeks back into the bathroom and backs out quickly.*

I'M FINE.

DAWN. You need space. Got it.

DAWN *turns off the music. Shower's still running.*

We need to talk about you. WE NEED TO TALK ABOUT YOU.

LEO. NO WE DON'T.

DAWN. I'M THNKING WE SHOULD FILE A LAWSUIT.

LEO. SUE THE COPS?

DAWN. YEAH. FOR REAL. Sue the shit out of them. Then they would think fucking twice before shoving your face into the pavement for no reason. 'Ladies and gentlemen of the jury, Leo is an upstanding citizen, an artist whose work has been shown in art galleries.' I could represent you. Might be a conflict of interest but there's ways to get around that. You would win slam-dunk, done and dusted, no sweat. And if we didn't win, which is not a possibility but we gotta consider all the angles, if they didn't decide in our favor, then the firm wouldn't charge you a dime and we still would have sent a message DO NOT TREAD ON ME!

Her phone rings.

Shit. Work. WORK, HON. I'M ON THE PHONE!

She answers the call.

Hey, Frankie Junior! Oh. Hello, Mrs Watts. How are you and Frankie Junior doing this morning? Yes, Ma'am it is early. It's 6 a.m., Ma'am. You're worried? There's nothing to be worried about, Mrs Watts. All Frankie Junior has to do is tell the Judge what he's already told me. And he'll be fine. No, Ma'am, he can't have a guilty conscience, because he's not guilty. That's right. The cops are trying to catch the bad guys and Frankie is helping them. That is the deal. Of course I sleep easy, Mrs Watts. And you should too. Yes, that's right, I'm one of the good guys, well one of the good gals. Yes, he still has to appear in court. Don't cry, Mrs Watts. Frankie Jr won't go to jail. On my word of honor. Because he didn't do anything wrong. It's not 'wrong place, wrong time,' because he wasn't even there. Could you put Frankie on the phone, please? Thanks. Frankie Junior! Is it a yes? You don't want to tell me over the phone? You need to meet in person. Right. Sure. Meeting in person is always better. I can get there in an hour, sound good? Great. See you then.

DAWN *ends the call and moves to pack up her laptop and paperwork. Hesitantly getting ready.*

LEO *comes out of the bathroom. Towel wrapped around his waist and one over his upper body too.*

Let's see your face.

She looks at him. Takes another photograph.

Those assholes. We're going to press charges. They won't get away with this.

LEO. I got an idea. It's kind of out there. Kind of scary. It's a totally far-out idea that could solve everything.

DAWN. Does it involve suing them?

LEO. Not everything can be settled in court.

DAWN. I don't like the sound of that. What are you thinking. Tell me.

LEO. Not yet. It's either stupid or bullshit. It's totally out there. I dunno.

DAWN. I gotta meet up with Frankie and you're going to come.

LEO. No thanks.

DAWN. You're coming with me.

LEO. No thanks. Really.

She sits.

Is Frankie nervous?

DAWN. Very.

LEO. Go see him. I'm good.

DAWN *continues getting ready. Packing up her briefcase.*

DAWN. Should I meet him in sweatpants?

LEO. You look good in sweats.

DAWN. I'm gonna slip into something more professional. He'll feel more confident if I'm looking the part.

She goes to change.

LEO *stands in the middle of the room, not even attempting to dry himself.*

DAWN *moves in and out of the bedroom and bathroom, keeping the conversation going as she puts on work clothes and does her hair and make-up.*

You're coming with me.

LEO. My presence would violate your lawyer–client privilege.

DAWN. We're meeting at the diner. You could sit at another table while we talk.

LEO. I'm ok.

DAWN. They pushed you down and your face hit the street. That's criminal. You could also charge them with violating your civil rights. You were just walking down the street. And they roughed you up for no reason. Don't post the photos, that could compromise your case.

LEO. I won't post the photos.

ACT ONE, SCENE TWO 19

DAWN. Good.
  (*Rest.*)
  You shouldn't just sit here alone. I'll text Ralph. He'll come over.

She's typing the text.

LEO. Don't. I don't need him in my face right now. Besides, if he comes, Misha will come with him and I need to be alone.

DAWN. You need your friends around you.

LEO. I don't.

DAWN. I'll tell him to come over by himself.

LEO. Lemme just be, K?

  DAWN *stops texting. Puts her phone away.*

  Ralph is about to get that job. His big fancy University tenure-track gig. And Misha with her *Show* –

DAWN. It's blowing up. She's got followers. You should tune in. Especially today.

LEO. Ok, I'll watch Misha's Show.

DAWN. There you go. Good. Misha and Ralph. They're both doing great.

LEO. And we're not?

DAWN. We're doing great too, babe.

LEO
DAWN

  Looks of love between them, then when DAWN *worries over* LEO*'s face, he turns her away from obsessing over him so that she can check her own look in the mirror.*

DAWN. 'Frankie Junior. You are innocent. Kleinman, Hellerman, Joblotnik and Merse, we've got your back.'

LEO. You should be wearing a cape. Like the partners do on the commercial.

DAWN. Except that I'm not a partner.

LEO. You should be.

DAWN. Your lips to god's ears. In the meantime, I'm just one of the good-guy underlings in a firm full of ambulance-chasing sleazeballs.

LEO. You're showing them the better way.

DAWN. Infiltrate and educate. I'm trying to.
(*Rest.*)
You came home I woke up and I screamed and I know you hated that but your face – . At least you aren't hurt really bad. That would have been the worst.

LEO. You know all those studies that say one of the best places to get great ideas is when you're taking a shower and all the showers I've ever taken, and I've never gotten any ideas during said showers ever, but just now, I did. I got an idea. It's a Eureka moment.

DAWN. Tell me.

DAWN *gives the briefest glance to her watch, checking the time. She sits. Ready to listen.*

LEO. You're beautiful.

DAWN. Tell me. I wanna help.

LEO. I should let it marinate in my head. It's not really formed yet. It's formed but not totally. It's like a first draft of an idea and I'm needing to/

DAWN. /Let it marinate/

LEO. /Keep it cooking/

DAWN. /Stew/

LEO. /Yeah/

DAWN. /Cool./

LEO *gets up, going to the bedroom, getting his clothes. Then he goes back in the bathroom.*

What are you doing?

ACT ONE, SCENE TWO   21

LEO. I'm getting dressed.

DAWN. In the bathroom? You ok?

LEO. I'm fine.

He comes back in the room to finish putting on his clothes.

[DAWN. You should call your mom. You don't have to tell her anything. Just shoot the shit. She'll be glad to hear from you.

LEO. No she won't.

DAWN. She misses you.

LEO. She has Jesus.

DAWN. She texts me every day 'Tell Leo his mother misses him,' she says.

LEO. She joined a cult.

DAWN. She lives in a religious community.]

LEO (*rest*). Maybe cause I'm an insomniac who comes from a broken home. Maybe that's why the cops hassled me.

DAWN. Let go of that, huh? They hassled you cause they're assholes.

LEO. Maybe if I had had a better relationship with my father.

DAWN. Your father had a heart attack and died when you were 12. What happened to you is in no way your fault. I'm texting Ralph.

LEO. <u>Don't</u>.
   (*Rest.*)
   Was your client, Junior –

DAWN. Frankie Junior –

LEO. When you talked to him, on the phone, was he crying?

DAWN. Yeah. How'd you know?

LEO. You get a certain look on your face when you've been with someone who's been crying. Like you want to cry too, but you don't want to cry cause you're the one they're counting on to fix whatever stupid thing is making them cry. You care. That's what I love about you.

DAWN. I love you too.

Her phone sounds. A text. She looks at it.

Frankie wants to meet at his house cause his mom wants to meet too and she doesn't leave the house. Geeze. Come with me.

LEO. I'll be ok here. Although my tooth is loose or cracked or something.

She takes another photo of his face.

DAWN. I'll have to go into the office after, but we'll check in during the day and please call me for any reason. And I'll get a hold of my dentist, make you an appointment, and send a car to take you there, K?

LEO. I thought they were going to shoot me. I thought, I'm going to be one of those guys that they shoot.

DAWN *wraps her arms around* LEO, *hugging him. He pulls away.*

DAWN. You need justice. And lots of hugs. What are you doing?

LEO. I'm sitting. I'm just sitting in a chair. I'm just a black man sitting in a red chair.

DAWN. You're being in the moment. Good for you.
(*Rest.*)
What were you doing in that neighborhood anyway?

LEO
DAWN
LEO
DAWN

DAWN. I'm sorry. Do you accept my apology?

LEO. Yeah.

DAWN. A bunch of bad things happened to you.

LEO. Technically, a bunch of bad things did not happen to me. I don't want justice because I have justice. I've got perfect peace. I am not a victim. I am not one of those brothers done wrong by the man. I'm not one of those black men whose name they shout in the street cause he got gunned down for nothing. For NOTHING. Or, if he doesn't die, he gets to have his whole fucking life defined by his quest for justice and the most he gets out of it is some monetary settlement or some biopic. 'Framed By Injustice.' Can you see the movie? Brother under the thumb of the Man, then he's liberated by some nice white Lady lawyer. Oh – sorry. Do you accept my apology?

DAWN. Yes.

LEO. See? We're good.
(Rest.)
I just want to live my life.
(Rest.)
I was imagining –

DAWN. Your idea from the shower?

LEO. No. Forget that. When I was out walking last night. Couldn't sleep. Couldn't work. So I walked. On the street. A starry summer night. The smell of asphalt and perspiration and possibility. I could see the stars. A couple of them. Even with the street lights. And I had this flash: I. Am. Going. To. Make. It. I wasn't tripping. I was imagining. I was walking down the street and I was imagining. Dreaming, you could say. Where will I live when I make it? Usually I just walk around our block. And the winos on the stoops they all know me. And the coffee-shop guys on the corner, they wave. But tonight, when I was laying next to you, I was tossing and turning and I got up and I thought, I need to expand, you know. Maybe I'm restless cause I don't think big enough maybe, you know? Walking around and around our block is too much like a hamster on a wheel. So I walked over to the East Side. Where I cannot as yet afford to purchase a home or even rent. But when I make it, and I will, and I was thinking:

the brownstone or the limestone? Condo or Co-op? Something with lots of light and an outdoor space. A balcony, or, gosh, maybe even a rooftop garden. And, of course, getting something with a doorman is the smart way to go. A doorman building with a full-time maintenance staff on hand because then you don't have to spend your time fixing every little thing. That's the kind of place. We could splurge.

DAWN. We?

LEO. Yeah. Well. Shit.

LEO takes a ring box out of his pocket. Gets down on one knee. Opens the box. Lovely ring inside.

DAWN. It's beautiful. This is beautiful. I don't know what to say.

LEO. Dawn. Babe. Would you marry me?

DAWN. I don't know what to say.

LEO. Yes?

DAWN. I don't know what to say. It's a lot. This whole day. It's a lot. And it's still early.

LEO. You're saying it should be a bigger rock.

DAWN. Not at all.

LEO. You're saying no.

DAWN. I'm saying it's a lot. I'm saying a lot is happening. Today. I'm saying, let's just be like we are.

LEO. What are we like?

DAWN. This is your idea from the shower?

LEO. No. Forget about that. This, I had this planned for weeks. I was going to do it later today, well tonight. I was going to do it at the Spot. Weeks ago you were sleeping and I of course wasn't and I tied a little piece of thread around your finger and then took it to the jeweler's to make sure I had the size right. So I know it fits. Put it on and see. I was thinking it'd be fun to propose at the Spot and Misha and Ralph could, like cheer us on, but now I'm feeling like, now's the time, right?

DAWN. You were going to ask me in front of Misha and Ralph?

LEO. I was thinking they could help us make it festive.

DAWN. You're traumatized. You were stopped by the cops and you were mistreated and they pushed your face into the sidewalk and you wet your pants and it's only natural, that now, you want to get married.

LEO
DAWN

She checks her phone. LEO *gets off his bended knee. She touches* LEO*'s face.*

LEO. Say yes.

DAWN. Let's revisit this later, ok Babe?

LEO. Sure.

They kiss. DAWN *exits.*

LEO, *left alone, sits in that red chair. He's fighting back the tears.*

Scene Three: Misha and Ralph

A few hours later.

A nicer apartment in a nicer part of town. Colorful walls, multi-ethnic folk art, a cozy upbeat vibe.

MISHA*'s Show has a simple set-up: modest video camera and a laptop with a ring-light.* MISHA *would like to be starting her Show, instead she's watching* RALPH *as he stares blankly into space.*

RALPH. I'm in the Dustbowl, you know, in the 1930s. And I feel like my car is off the road and other cars are passing me by, just passing me by. There they all go, but I'm on the side of the road in a dusty ditch, cause there hasn't been water in ages, and my mouth is open and my mouth is full of dust and everybody on the road, they're all going to California. This is a sepia-toned silent movie. And I fall to the ground, beside my rusted little Model T, held together with borrowed string and broken dreams, and I lay there sobbing in the heat and this is my life. Before the Great Curtain falls.

MISHA. Babe? I'm guessing that they gave your job to someone else.

RALPH

RALPH

MISHA. Babe?

RALPH. Yeah?

MISHA. You didn't get the job?

RALPH. Nope.

MISHA. Want to talk about it?

RALPH. When is your Show?

MISHA *gives a glance at her phone, checking the time.*

MISHA. In like 3 minutes.

RALPH. I can wait.

MISHA. You sure?

RALPH. Yep. Nope. Yep yep. Yes. I'm sure. I am sure that I can wait.

MISHA. We'll talk after and we'll totally sort it out.

RALPH. Sounds good. Do your Show. You go, girl! I'll watch. I'll – I'll monitor the livestream. Like I always do. And then/

MISHA. /And then we'll figure out your job thing.

RALPH. It's not a 'job thing.' It's a 'no-job-no-thing.'

MISHA. Sure you don't wanna talk now?

RALPH. No. You've got your Show.

MISHA. Right. Sorry. I mean/

RALPH. /Want me to fix the light?

MISHA. I did it ok.

RALPH. I'll fix the light. I always fix the light.

RALPH helps organize the lighting.

MISHA. Why don't you give Leo a call? You guys could have one of your bro-talks. That would help.

RALPH. Maybe. But, maybe not. Who knows? Leo and his sleepless thing. Please. Just run the opening and I'll check the camera. Go on. I'm fine.

MISHA. It's going to be ok, babe.

MISHA gets in her spot. RALPH fiddles with the lights and then fiddles with the camera.

RALPH. Go.

MISHA. Morning, People! I'm Misha and welcome to 'Ask A Black.' Where someone like you can feel free to ask something of someone like me.
(*Rest.*)
How was that?

RALPH is looking at the light.

Do I need more light?

RALPH. Background's blown out I'm on it.

MISHA. Thanks.

He turns off a lamp behind her. Maybe pulls down the blinds. While MISHA powders her nose, checks her hair and clothes.

Is the intro clip running?

RALPH checks his computer.

RALPH. Intro clip is rolling and the call-in number is on the screen. Plus, you look great. You got 30 seconds.

MISHA *checks her special call-in line. It's <u>an old school red rotary phone</u>.*

You are the most beautiful and the most righteous woman on the planet.

MISHA. And you're my knight in shining armor.

RALPH. Showtime.

MISHA motions for RALPH to sit on the couch and rest. He does so, watching her livestream from his computer.

The instrumental portion of 'Your Love To Love Me' plays and MISHA speaks her intro over it.

MISHA. *Gooood* Morning, People! Misha's in your house! Welcome back to 'Ask A Black.' We livestream once a week, every Thursday morning, cause we want someone like <u>you</u> to feel free to share whatever's on your mind with someone like <u>me</u>.
(*Rest.*)
You'll be heard
But you won't be seen!
Give Misha a call
At the number on the screen!

She turns off the intro music.

The red telephone rings. She's got a caller on the line. She answers it.

Hey there, this is Misha, welcome to 'Ask A Black.'

DEBBIE FROM ST LOUIS. Yeah, I just want to know how come people get offended when I ask them if I can touch their hair?

MISHA. Our first caller of the day is starting off with a big question. That's a great question, Caller #1.

DEBBIE FROM ST LOUIS. I'm Debbie from St Louis. And, I mean, I wouldn't mind if someone wanted to touch <u>my</u> hair.

MISHA. If we were hanging out, and if you wanted to touch my hair, I probably wouldn't mind either.

ACT ONE, SCENE THREE 29

DEBBIE FROM ST LOUIS. But, my friends, my black friends, they don't like it when I ask.

MISHA. You've got black friends.

DEBBIE FROM ST LOUIS. More than one. And I'm not black, of course.

MISHA. Yeah, that would have been my guess.

RALPH's sitting on the couch working hard to keep his cool. MISHA glances at RALPH but keeps focused on her Show.

Debbie, to answer your question about the hair, it's all about personal space. Each of us has a right to our personal space and, the more familiar you are with somebody, the more negotiable that space is. So, just realize that, touching somebody is a big deal, put yourself in that person's shoes, be ok with 'no' for an answer and, yeah, take it from there.

DEBBIE FROM ST LOUIS. Ok. Thanks!

The call ends.

RALPH is struggling in silence.

MISHA (*to* RALPH). You ok?

RALPH. I'm great.

The red telephone rings again.

MISHA. We've got another caller. Hi there! Welcome to 'Ask A Black.'

Meanwhile, RALPH *sits again. Trying to stay cool. He's really on edge.*

MIKE FROM BIRMINGHAM. Hi this is Mike from Birmingham. Do you think we're going to have a race-war any time soon? I'm thinking, the way things are going, it's just a matter of time.

MISHA. I'm thinking One Love, right?

MIKE FROM BIRMINGHAM. Maybe. Prepare yourself.

The line goes dead. And then starts ringing again right away.

MISHA. Whatever your color we gotta stick together. Like MLK said 'lots of us came on different ships, but we're all in the same boat now.'

She answers the phone.

You're on 'Ask A Black.'

JACK FROM ATLANTA. I got hassled by the cops last night.

RALPH *thinks he recognizes* LEO*'s voice.*

RALPH. Is that Leo?

JACK FROM ATLANTA. My name is Jack and I'm from Atlanta.

RALPH. It sounds like Leo.

MISHA *doubts it's* LEO. *And, if it is* LEO, *it doesn't sound like him.*

MISHA. Hey there, Jack from Atlanta, talk to me. You're a brother, right?

JACK FROM ATLANTA. Does it matter?

MISHA. Not at all. Jack, this is a serious topic. The cops are off the chain these days, right? If you haven't already, you need to get a lawyer. You need to talk with your pastor or therapist, and you need to talk with your friends.

Meanwhile, RALPH *is really on-edge.*

JACK FROM ATLANTA. The world is breaking my spirit, you know? And I gotta take some kind of action. I gotta do something to somehow extricate myself from the abyss. You know what I'm saying? I feel like I'm about to do something crazy.

MISHA. Crazy like what?

RALPH, *agitated for his own reasons, sits again. Trying to stay cool.*

JACK FROM ATLANTA. My options for making it through the day have been severely curtailed because of this shit.

ACT ONE, SCENE THREE   31

RALPH *seems calm. For now.*

MISHA. I hear you, man. The pain is real.

JACK FROM ATLANTA. I am going to have a conversation with a lawyer.

MISHA. Good idea, man.

The line goes dead.

The hotline starts ringing right away. MISHA *doesn't answer immediately.*

(*To her audience.*) People, that is a very intense situation. Jack, you've got our prayers.

She answers the phone.

Hey there, you're on 'Ask A Black.'

ROBERTA FROM PORTLAND. I'm Roberta. I'm calling from Portland. Did you know, back in the day, that there were laws that <u>banned</u> black people from entering the state of Oregon?

MISHA. I'm aware of that, Roberta. So what's your question?

ROBERTA FROM PORTLAND. No question, I just wanted to share that information with your audience.

MISHA. And we thank you for that.

ROBERTA FROM PORTLAND. Thanks for listening!

MISHA *hangs up.*

Meanwhile, across the room, RALPH *makes a phone call.* MISHA's *hotline rings. She doesn't answer right away.*

MISHA. Before I take my next caller, I want to remind you that we stream 'Ask A Black' every Thursday morning at 8 a.m. so you can get the deal, and start to heal, before you get on the job, or behind the wheel. I'm your host Misha, reminding you to keep it cool, keep it real, go for broke and please stay woke.
(*Rest.*)
Hey, caller, this is Misha.

32   WHITE NOISE

RALPH *is her next caller. <u>He tries to disguise his voice</u>.*

RALPH. I got passed over for a promotion.

MISHA *gives a look to* RALPH. *She knows it's him.*

MISHA. I'm sorry to hear that. What's your name, friend?

RALPH. I'm Joe. From Jersey.

MISHA. So, 'Joe,' you got passed over/

RALPH. /They passed me over in favor of this guy from, like, India.

MISHA. My Show's called 'Ask A Black,' so, how can I, being who I am, help you with what you're going through?

RALPH. The motherfucking asshole from India got my goddamn job cause –

MISHA. On 'Ask A Black' we ask all our callers to refrain from that kind of language.

The line goes dead.

MISHA *gives a look to* RALPH.

RALPH *takes a pillow from the couch and stifles a scream.* RALPH *is having a hard time.* MISHA *stays focused on her Show. She gets another phone call.*

Who are we talking with?

ELAINE FROM TORONTO. Hi! My name's Elaine! I'm calling from Toronto!

MISHA. Elaine from Toronto! Welcome to the Show!

ELAINE FROM TORONTO. I just adopted a little boy. And he's black.

MISHA. And you're wondering –

Across the room, RALPH, <u>screaming, rips the modem out of the wall. He also yanks out the lights and</u> phone, <u>totally shutting down the Show</u>.

ACT ONE, SCENE THREE   33

RALPH. AAAAAAH/

MISHA. /What the fuck, Ralph?/

RALPH. /AAAAAAH/

MISHA. /USE YOUR WORDS!/

RALPH. /I NEED TO TALK./

MISHA. /YOU SAID YOU COULD WAIT! FUCK YOU!/

RALPH. I'm sorry! You're angry! I mean, I'm not sorry that you're angry. I support your anger! I've always supported your anger! I've always had your back! But I'm having a hard time right here!

MISHA. Ok. Talk to me.

RALPH. I'm the one they promised the job to. I'm qualified. Tenure would have been sweet. I deserve it. But they gave it to someone else. Someone who writes *sonnets*. A fucking Shakespeare-wannabe. What do you think of that?

MISHA. I think it sucks. But there's lots of factors that go into deciding –

RALPH. You're saying he should have gotten the job? The other guy instead of me?

MISHA. It might be that 'publish or perish' kind of thing.

RALPH. So, I don't get <u>published</u>. So what. I write great stuff that keeps getting passed over. That keeps getting put on the 'No thank you,' pile. I got a file cabinet full of rejection letters, but I'm a great <u>teacher</u>. And the job is a <u>teaching job</u>, so, so what that I haven't been writing anything for the past five years? And so what if they all know it?
(*Rest.*)
Goddamn bullshit is what it is! I was teaching great! I was working hard! I worked my ass off! And would they give me the promotion?! Hell no!

He stops venting and just holds the table and breathes.
MISHA*'s with him as much as she can be.*

That job, it had my name on it. The Dean, he promised it to me. Saying, of course, it would have to be approved by the Committee. But I was totally his pick. Last week they were all talking to me about what kind of furniture I wanted in my office! They gave me their *word*. I will kill them all.

MISHA. Hon?

RALPH. What.
(*Rest.*)
Ok, I won't kill them.

MISHA. How can I help?

RALPH. You can't help. Life hates me.

MISHA *hugs* RALPH.

MISHA. I'm sorry.

RALPH. It's not your fault.
(*Rest.*)
You know what kind of furniture I wanted? Swedish Modern.

MISHA. I'm so sorry, babe.

RALPH. Yeah. Whatever. I'll just be Mr Unpublished-Part-Time-Professor for the rest of my life. I'll just be nobody. I'll just be nothing. That was the only thing that both of my parents could ever agree on.

MISHA. Tonight we're going to the Spot with Leo and Dawn. That'll be good, right?

RALPH. I don't want to tell them about it. This was going to be my big break.

MISHA. It's not like you need the money.

RALPH. I was going to break free of my family's shit. I was going to make it on my own steam and this was going to be my moment.

MISHA. You'll have your moment.

RALPH. Jagannath got the job.

MISHA. I figured.

RALPH. Jagannath, he's not from India. He's from Sri Lanka. He's dark-skinned and identifies as black. Which, yeah, ok. His prerogative, ok. And he's always talking about the Tamil Tigers. The Liberation Tigers of Tamil Eelam. And how they're like the Black Panthers which <u>somehow</u> gives him some faux Black Power Cred which is some bullshit. It's so totally annoying.

MISHA. Yeah, it's totally annoying.

RALPH. It's fucked up.

MISHA. It's fucked up.

RALPH. I should gotten that job.

MISHA. But you didn't.

RALPH. A second-rate person has my job just because that second-rate person is black.

MISHA
RALPH

RALPH. I thought that's where we were going with it. I really thought that's where we were going with it.

MISHA. You were going there, and you went there all alone.

RALPH. So, I'm all alone now? Do I look old?

MISHA. You look great. You're my knight in shining armor.

RALPH. And you're the most righteous woman on the planet.

MISHA. You should call Leo.

RALPH. We'll see them tonight, K?

MISHA. Sure.

RALPH. I have this fear. In my stomach. And my feet. The skin on my feet is crawling. And the ground underfoot is shifting. And I don't know who I am. And the only thing I know is that I know the horrible truth: Life. Hates. Me.

MISHA *slaps him. Hard.*

MISHA. You are not going there. You are going somewhere else. You are not going to wallow. You are not going to sulk. This is not a pity party. You are my shining knight. Your students call you 'Righteous Ralph.' You are – we are going to go somewhere else. We are going to do something else. Something. We are going to –

RALPH. Fuck. Wanna fuck?

MISHA. Right. Ok. Let's go there.

Things heat up to Sex.

Scene Four: At the Spot

After hours at a gun-shooting range. It's got a plain utilitarian vibe. Not 'red-necky.' Just an establishment that's well maintained, serviceable but drab. Paper targets in the far distance.

DAWN*'s wearing her eye and ear protection (pulled down) along with a kitschy cowboy shirt. She should be loading her gun, a brownish Beretta, and taking her turn. But instead, gun in one hand and bullet-magazine in the other, she's just standing there [talking to herself].*

[DAWN. I hate shooting. Because – because it's loud. And violent. Every time we meet up here at the Spot, the gun range, I try to have a good time. And I've done everything I can to get into it. Everything in my power. Back in college, I took lessons. Shooting lessons. And, yeah, I know what you're thinking. But it was actually inspiring. My Instructor. A woman, talked to me about the beauty of firearms while she made butterfly-blue herbal tea in her great-grandmother's silver samovar. The guns had brand names: the Berettas, the Kolibris, the Defenders, the Hardballers, Tomcat, Cheetah,

Storm and Thunder. The Brownings, the Colts, the Glocks and the Hecklers. Liliputs and Lugers. Jerichos and Kimbers. Mambas, Magnums, Remmingtons. Smith & Wessons, Webley & Scotts. Welrods. Uzis. She had been shot once. In the face. By her ex-husband. And since that day, guns were her thing. She had the most beautiful smile, and a voice that sounded like singing. Plus she knew everything about guns. Makes. Models. History. First thing she did when I came to learn was: she gave me a little red pocket-size copy of the Constitution of the United States. Asked me if I knew what the 2nd Amendment was. 'The right to bear arms,' duh. Then she asked me what it <u>meant</u>. 'If you don't know your rights you'll lose them,' she said. She had me practice for hours. Showed me how to clean a pistol. She was a stickler for gun safety. 'Always treat your gun as if it's loaded.' 'Keep your gun unloaded. And only load it when you're ready to use it.' 'Only have your finger on the trigger when you're pointing your gun down-range and are prepared to shoot.' When I wanted her to talk with me about the politics of gun violence, instead of talking, she would just touch her face, tracing her scar. But we've gotta talk about it right? Well, we didn't, so I guess not. The Gun Lady was the most inspiring teacher I've ever had. And still, no matter how hard I try, I still can't 'get it on the paper' as they say. I hit everything down-range BUT the target. I'm not good at shooting. Because it's violent. And violence is often unjust, and me, I'm all about justice. Plus, at the end of the day, whatever color you <u>paint</u> your gun it's always just going to look like a penis.]

Lights up on the others. LEO, MISHA *and* RALPH. *They're all wearing matching kitschy cowboy shirts.* RALPH *has brought a bottle of Scorpion Mescal.*

They holler at DAWN, *egging her on.*

I'm warming up!

MISHA. We're waiting.

RALPH. I'll take your turn.

DAWN. We forget that a bullet can pierce a body.

LEO. If you hate it, you should sit it out.

DAWN. If I sit it out then we won't have a thing. Shooting guns is our thing.

MISHA. We can get another thing.

DAWN. But it won't be as intense.

MISHA. Yeah, cause guns are deep.

LEO. Guns are dope.

RALPH. Guns are sacred. And magical. And fucked up.

DAWN. When we're each 100 years old –

RALPH. We'll all be in the same old folks' home which will have a built-in gun range.

LEO. Speak for yourself, man. I'm going to – I don't know what, but I'm going to be someplace where it's happening.

MISHA. At a hundred?

LEO. It ain't a crime to dream.

DAWN. You're right, babe. Dreaming is not a crime.

But still, DAWN *is hasn't yet taken her shot.*

MISHA. We could start the band back up again. That was a thing.

Together they sing. They even fall into a bit of air-band choreography. DAWN *as the drummer,* MISHA *on bass,* LEO *on rhythm guitar and* RALPH *on lead guitar.*

DAWN/MISHA/LEO/RALPH. ALL I WANT
ALL I WANT, YEAH
ALL I WANT
I JUST WANT YOUR LOVE TO LOVE ME.

It's their happy place. It's a good time. And then it's over.

RALPH. I'm glad we quit the band.

MISHA. Me too.

LEO. Me too.

DAWN. Me too. It was so – emotional.

RALPH. I'll do your turn. Give me the gun.

DAWN. No. I'm committed to this. I've put like 10 years into this. Ever since college. Trying to keep up with you guys. I've taken lessons./

LEO. /You studied with the Gun Lady./

DAWN. /I have a trigger-hand glove. I have pistol-shooting shoes.

RALPH. I'll buy you gloves and shoes for something else.

MISHA. Throwing your money around is not the answer to everything, babe.

LEO. He was only trying to help.

DAWN. I don't want stuff for something else. I just wanna get good at it. That's not too much to ask.

RALPH (*to* LEO). Bro, if you really fell in the shower, then how come the side of your face looks more like you hit the pavement?

LEO. Cause our shower is rough. It's got those rough tiles. Cause we don't live high on the hog. What can I tell you, man, we can't all be Ralph punching the clock as a college professor, but really he grew up as a trust-fund kid.

RALPH. I didn't.

LEO. I know. And your old man was an asshole. I was just talking out the side of my neck. Sorry.

RALPH. 'Hit It And Quit It!' Can we do this? Please?

DAWN. Ok. I'm just gonna shoot this gun.

She pulls up her safety gear, then, loading her gun and aiming it down-range, double-handed, she finally takes her shot.

Fuck.

MISHA. You suck.

DAWN. That's not news.

DAWN looks down-range, studying the paper target.

I didn't even hit the paper. I'm hopeless.

DAWN ejects the magazine.

RALPH. For real, bro, what happened to your face?

DAWN. Maybe not 'what happened' but what are we going to do about it.

MISHA chooses a gun and, gun still unloaded, gets ready to take her turn. She's got some style.

MISHA. What happened?

LEO. Nothing.

DAWN. Leo had a far-out idea in the shower and now we've got a gameplan, right babe?

LEO. Right.

MISHA. You guys got engaged.

RALPH. You guys got pregnant.

LEO. No no no.

RALPH. That was three 'nos' but we only made two guesses.

MISHA. You're moving. To another city.

RALPH. Move to another city and I'll kill you. You guys aren't moving, are you?

DAWN. We're not moving.

RALPH. You got married.

MISHA. You went to city hall and got married which is totally not fair cause we were all going to get married together. You guys weren't even engaged last week. This is some bullshit. You went and got married without us?

ACT ONE, SCENE FOUR   41

Angrily, MISHA *loads and takes her shot. She's pleased.*

LEO. We're not married.

MISHA. But you're engaged.

DAWN
LEO

> MISHA *retrieves the paper target by yanking a pulley and hauling the series of circles into view.*

MISHA. Bullseye. Almost. Not bad.

DAWN. At least you hit the paper.

RALPH. Last week you were 'getting engaged any minute.' Me and you, bro, we were talking rings. Now you're taking a step back? You're – you guys are breaking up! Shit.

LEO. It's nothing like that.

RALPH. Did you buy her that ring, bro?

DAWN. How are you guys doing?

MISHA. We're great./

RALPH. /Perfection.

LEO. You hear about that job yet?

RALPH. Nope. Not yet.

MISHA. Yeah. Dawn, how's your case?

DAWN. Going great. How's your Show?

MISHA. It's gonna get picked up by a network any minute.

RALPH. How's your work going, bro?

LEO. Slow.

RALPH. But, cause you're not sleeping, you're working through the night, right? Damn, if I had your problem, I would have written, like, 10 novels by now.

MISHA. Or at least one. Start small.

RALPH. How about I get you another noise-maker.

LEO. No thanks.

RALPH. But you still can't sleep.

LEO. What can I tell you. I'm stressed but it's all good. And, maybe, maybe, I am sleeping right now. Maybe this is a dream and you're all a part of it.

RALPH *pinches* LEO.

Ow!

RALPH. Have you started those self-portraits? Say yes.

LEO. No. But, not to worry. It's all good.

DAWN. Tell them your big new idea.

RALPH. Yeah, spill it!

LEO. I'll spill it when the time is right.

RALPH. Which will be – ?

LEO. When I've had a drink.

RALPH *opens the bottle and hands it to* LEO.

[DAWN (*to* LEO). When we're at the range we drink in moderation.]

MISHA. Yeah, safety first.]

LEO *has already raised the bottle and taken a modest sip. He passes the bottle around. The others decline.*

LEO
LEO
LEO

MISHA. Don't you think it's weird, in all the years of coming here, we never come during regular business hours?

DAWN. I like that our special meet-up thing is private. I mean, until I get good at it.

RALPH. If you guys want to come during regular hours, and deal with the crowds, go ahead.

MISHA. We could join a league.

LEO. That's cause you weren't on the team in college. I told you to join the girls' team – or at least try out.

RALPH. How many trophies and division championships did we rack up for the school, bro?

LEO. Too many, bro!

RALPH. And how many times did my dad <u>never</u> come see me shoot?

LEO. Don't even go there. It's not worth it. Drink.

RALPH and LEO drink, still modestly sipping, though.

MISHA (*to* DAWN). If you joined a league now would you join a women's or a co-ed?

DAWN. Women's. Def.

RALPH. Coming in during the day would remind me of my so-called father, so I am more than content just to keep a set of keys, and come and go when I please.

LEO. But not bad right, the luxurious economic security generated by your having inherited a piece of real estate on which sits an established shooting range with a robust clientele. Your shit's fucked up but at least you're making some money from it.

RALPH. Shoot. Somebody shoot.

LEO goes to the table to choose his pistol. Selects one. Handles it. Loads it. Very mindful. Very methodical. Completely devoid of swagger. Then he stands in position. Gun pointed down-range. Very Zen. He shoots. Single handed. Hits his mark.

LEO. YES, BABY! YES! YOU SAW IT! SHONUFF! WHO IS THE SHOOTING CHAMP? LEO! WHO IS AT HOME ON THE RANGE?! LEO. I AM THE PISTOL KING! I AM THE TOP GUN!

RALPH. Let's see if my man can make two in a row. Do we have the ladies' permission?

DAWN *and* MISHA. Go for it.

LEO. Will do! Can do!

LEO gets ready to shoot again. Standing at the line again, very Zen. RALPH *encourages him, kind of like a low-key coach.*

RALPH. Come on, hot shot, show us what you got.

DAWN. If we started something new today, when we turn, say 50, we would have been at it longer than we've been at this.

MISHA. What could possibly be more fascinating than this?

RALPH. Steady your mind and line up your sights. Front-sight-back-sight. You know what I'm talking about.

LEO *shoots again. Another bullseye.*

LEO *ceremoniously unloads his gun and places it on the table while* RALPH, *with equal ceremony, retrieves the target by yanking a pulley and hauling the paper target into view.*

Continuing the ceremony, LEO *and* RALPH *study the paper target.* LEO*'s hit two bullseyes.*

Then LEO *and* RALPH *do a series of weird slow-motion and silent sports-victory moves: high-fives, chest-bumps and more.*

The women watch the men.

MISHA. If I were an anthropologist, you guys would be interesting.

LEO. Speaking of anthropology, Meesh, what happened on your Show today?

MISHA. You watched my Show?

LEO. Yeah and your video-feed went down towards the end.

RALPH. Technical difficulties. Totally my bad.
(*Rest.*)
Bro, you called in today, didn't you?

LEO (*rest*). I did.

DAWN. You called in? To her Show?

MISHA. That's how come your face/

RALPH. /The cops hit you/

LEO. Actually the sidewalk hit me but they, yeah, the cops gave me a push.

RALPH *and* MISHA. You're fucking kidding, man./ Are you okay?

LEO. Same old shit. Felt good to call in and talk about it, even for a quick minute, Meesh.

MISHA. I'm glad the Show helped.

RALPH. You're going to sue, right?

MISHA. Of course you will.

DAWN. He met with a lawyer today.

LEO. That I did.

MISHA. Good. And, if you need to talk some more, you don't have to call my Show.

LEO. My shit is messed up, but it's not nearly as bad as that other guy who called in. Joe from Jersey.

MISHA. Yeah. He was, a, yeah.

RALPH. 'Joe from Jersey.'

MISHA. What do you expect?

DAWN. I'm not going to stereotype all men named Joseph from New Jersey.

LEO (*to* DAWN). He was this angry dude thinking he didn't get hired cause of reverse discrimination.

DAWN. Geeze.

LEO. He was yelling like –

RALPH. He wasn't yelling.

LEO. Well, you know, you've heard those nutjobs.

DAWN. Sounds like he lost it.

MISHA. Bless his heart.

RALPH. For me, when bad things happen, I just do my best to roll with it. Cause I know my ship will come in sooner or later.

LEO. That's your privilege talking.

DAWN. We could also call it Ralph's optimism.

LEO. But, what if you weren't optimistically privileged?

RALPH. I'd probably do something crazy.

MISHA. Like kill somebody.

LEO. I'd do something crazier than that.

DAWN. Like – ?

LEO. I've got an idea that's pretty far-out.
   (*Rest.*)
   Wait for it.

MISHA. Standing by.

RALPH. Drumroll.

> DAWN *does a drumroll on the table. Drumming increases in speed. This next section starts out feeling innocuous and playful. It builds in gravity and intensity.*

LEO. Ralph?

RALPH. Bro?

LEO. I want you to buy me.

RALPH. Buy you what?

LEO. Buy me, me. Buy me.

MISHA. That's funny. Ha ha.

DAWN. More like funny weird.

RALPH. I'm laughing. Inside.

LEO. I'm for real.

DAWN. This is your far-out idea? Your revelation in the shower? It's totally offensive –

MISHA. But I'm not sure to whom.

RALPH. I am at a loss for words. I am speechless.

LEO. Buy me. Make me your property.

RALPH. No. Hey. Shake it off. I feel your pain, but let's – shoot it out. Shoot it out of your system, right? Release the tension. Stand on the line, point down-range and give me 5 on the money.

LEO does so and shoots 5 rounds fast.

Great shots, bro! Really! And, you feel better, right? How about 5 more?

LEO. No. Actually – I feel more wound up.

LEO ejects the magazine and places the gun safely down.

RALPH. Talk therapy is what you need.

DAWN. You could go to Ralph's trainer. You could punch it out on the heavy bag.

MISHA. Or scream it out. That's what I do. In the subway. When the train's coming. You can scream and no one hears you. And, if you turn your face away from people, then nobody can see your mouth moving and then you just like, get on the train like nothing's up, you know.

LEO. AAAAAAAAAAAAAAAAAAAAAAH! AAAAAAAAAAAAAAAAH! AAAAAAAAAH!

RALPH
DAWN
MISHA
LEO
RALPH
MISHA
DAWN

MISHA. It's coming up, right? It's coming up and coming out.

LEO. No.
(*Rest.*)
Back in the day, a Guy like me would be walking wherever and he'd get stopped by the Law, some law-enforcement individual, and there would be a 'Whose nigger are you, nigger?' moment and the Guy like me would be like, 'I belong to Master So-And-So,' and the Law would be like 'Oh, if you're Master So-And-So's property, then you're cool with us, so go ahead on with your black self' and a Guy like me would be protected. A Guy like me would be safe. Cause he was <u>owned</u> by somebody. Cause the brother was the <u>property</u> of the man. He was safe cause he was/

MISHA. /Don't say it/

RALPH. /A Slave/

LEO. /Bingo/

MISHA. We're your friends. Friends don't let friends – what are you doing?

DAWN. What am I doing? I am looking around for the camera. Cause I know just what this is. This is 'Leo's Far-Out Idea.' When your gallery dropped you, and you said you're going to find something better to do. Something more relevant. 'Self-portraits.' And this is it, right? You're doing that, that performance-art thing. And this is part of it. And we're all going to show up in some video, right?

RALPH. You're such a lawyer.

DAWN. And why is that a problem? I have clients who depend on me. You write things that nobody ever reads!

MISHA. Drink something. Everybody drink something.

They pass the bottle around, this time each taking a deep swig.

LEO. First the lights come. And then their voices. Through that loudspeaker. 'Stand where you are and keep your hands visible.' And the first thing I thought was 'visible to whom?'

Because it's dark and I'm – dark – and of course I hold up
my hands and then I feel like ok, Leo, you are now one of
the chosen ones. You are now one of that select group of men
who walk down the street minding their own business and
get stopped for nothing. Wrong place wrong time. Unlucky.
My dad would tell me how to avoid these situations. My
mom would tell me. She had a brother who – but he was a
bad guy, see. He was trouble from day one. My parents and
me, we had The Talk. So I knew what I had to do to be a
good guy. Smile. Good school. Good grades. I'm not telling
you what you don't already know.

MISHA. Go on, man.

LEO. So I had this idea. Ralph, you're somebody. Yeah, ok, it's
cause of your dad, and this place you got, but, in the scheme
of things, you are a somebody, plus you got your academic
thing happening. My best buddy Ralph is a big somebody.
Come on, dog, admit it. You got lucky and you came into
money, and, also, by your own steam, right, you're going
places. So, I'm taking a shower, and it comes to me, that, the
only way I can be safe is to be <u>owned</u>. Be under the
protection of someone who, to the powers that be, is a Big
Somebody. And My Big Somebody would offer me a kind of
shelter. And should They stop me next time, I will have
something to say. Something that would give Them pause.
Make Them think. Make Them leave me be. Make Them
leave me the fuck alone. 'I belong to Ralph Shildkritter. Yes,
that Ralph Shildkritter. The one who inherited a big-ass
shooting range. Ralph Shildkritter, he looks after me. I am
his property. And if I am harmed, injured or disrespected in
any way, you, Mr Po-Lice, you gotta answer to Mr Ralph.'
So, Ralph, bro, in exchange for this Protection I'm talking
about, I will be your Enslaved Person.

RALPH. No thank you. I mean, I hear where you're coming
from, but – . No fucking way, right? You want us to go
around town with me telling the cops that I own you?

LEO. Yeah. You and me, Master Person and Enslaved Person,
walking the streets. Making a statement. Showing the world
how far we've <u>not</u> come!

RALPH. No way.

MISHA. You think playing the victim is going to help you?

LEO. I'm not playing the victim. I'm taking a stand.

DAWN. Because you got pushed down and hit your head?

RALPH. You need a bodyguard.

LEO. This shit goes deeper than that!

RALPH. So deep that you want to be the Slave and you want me to be the bad guy?

MISHA. The Master.

DAWN. Yeah, the bad guy.

RALPH. You'll get all the pity and I'll get all the shit. No thanks.

LEO. You're gonna say yes. You gotta say yes.
(*Rest.*)
Dawn, babe, I'll need you to look at the contract.

DAWN. What contract?

MISHA. There's not a contract cause there's not a deal.

RALPH (*to* DAWN *and* LEO). Are you guys going through some stuff?

LEO *and* DAWN. We're good/fine.

RALPH. If someone had videoed the cops beating you up –

LEO. They didn't beat me up.

MISHA. You hit the ground and your tooth is broken.

LEO. I got up and walked away.

RALPH. They roughed you up/

LEO. /They didn't rough, they didn't beat./

MISHA. /You're obviously traumatized/

DAWN. /That's what I said/

LEO. /I am fine.

DAWN *and* MISHA *and* RALPH. You want to be a slave!

LEO. HOW THE HELL ELSE AM I SUPPOSED TO PROTECT MYSELF?!
(*Rest.*)
What else can I do? Really. What else can I do?!
(*Rest.*)
THAT'S HOW BAD IT IS! THAT'S HOW BAD IT IS! THAT'S HOW BAD IT IS! AND ANYBODY WHO DOESN'T KNOW IT – YOU'RE JUST LYING TO YOURSELF!!
(*Rest.*)
I am of sound mind and body. But the shit is getting to me. And that's bad. Cause my whole life I've done everything right. Everything right but somehow everything ain't all right. And I hate that. And I hate them.

MISHA. Preach.

DAWN. I hear you, babe.

RALPH. Between the four of us, I am the closest thing to the 'white-patriarchy' thing. And so, I am willing to bear the burden of their less than appropriate behavior. And so I say, 'I'm sorry.' I am sorry. Will you accept my apology?

LEO. I accept your apology.

RALPH. Cool. Let's just shoot.

DAWN. Fine.

MISHA. Girls against boys.

RALPH. Because you want to lose?

LEO. I'm not letting go of this. I want to be a slave. Your slave, Ralph. Unless you can't bring yourself to do it.

MISHA. Is what Leo just said kinda hot, or is it just me?

DAWN. It's kind of hot.

MISHA. I wanna be your slave.

DAWN. I want you to own me.

MISHA. I want you to dominate me.

DAWN. What's our safe word?

MISHA. Our safe word is – Stop.

RALPH. That's funny.

LEO. I'm serious.

RALPH. Like what, you're daring me?

LEO. Righteous Ralph, I'm giving you the opportunity to transgress.

[MISHA. It's like 'Quantum Entanglement.'

RALPH. What?

DAWN. It's when things are connected –

MISHA. Even though they don't <u>appear</u> to be connected.]

LEO. I'm feeling like I want to be a slave and so, just maybe, Ralph, you just maybe might be feeling like you wanna be a master.

RALPH. But I don't. Do I?

LEO. I think you do. I feel like shit and I need <u>you</u> to help me to feel better.

MISHA. No you don't.

LEO. Yes I do.

DAWN. Stop.

RALPH. /Just for the sake of curiosity/

LEO. /for a limited time/

DAWN. Babe?

LEO. /And next time the cops get in my face for no reason/

RALPH. /We'll cross that bridge when we come to it.

ACT ONE, SCENE FOUR 53

DAWN. More like we'll burn that bridge when we come to it.

MISHA. Maybe you should buy a gun. You never wanted to own one, but –

LEO. You're kidding, right?

DAWN. Yeah, let's make him a black man with a gun.

MISHA. Bad idea, sorry. It's just feeling like this is one of those 'By Any Means Necessary' moments.

DAWN. Leo. Babe. If I'd of said 'yes' would you be doing this?

MISHA *and* RALPH. Said 'yes' to what?

LEO. <u>The cops fucked me up</u>! Bro, help me work through it.

RALPH. Sleep on it. Ask me again in the morning.

LEO. I don't sleep. Can't.

RALPH. Right.

LEO
RALPH

LEO *takes a contract from his bag. It's hefty.*

LEO. The lawyer drew it up. Check it out.

DAWN. That's why you went to the lawyer?

RALPH *reads it. They all crowd around and give it a look.*

RALPH. It's long.

LEO. It's got everything I need.

RALPH. I gotta read it before I sign it.

LEO. Trust me.

DAWN. This is a joke.

MISHA. You're fucking kidding, right?

LEO. I'm not. And the contract will make it official. It'll give us a framework, a playbook, a gameplan.

RALPH. Cause you don't trust me?

LEO. Cause I want us to agree on the specifics./

DAWN. /That's very modern./

MISHA. /And not at all historically accurate./

DAWN. You got a lawyer at my firm to draw this up?

LEO. For a fee.

MISHA. With all that's available to you, this is what you're doing? You could move out of the country, or join the Movement, or go to a rally, or march in the streets, or help pass a law, right?

LEO. But I no longer believe in the system.
(*Rest*.)
The promise of freedom is just some bullshit because the world don't support it. Black folks out there every day are falling prey to the anger, the unarticulated self-loathing, the unfathomable despair – so under the pressure, we end up doing a crime and getting locked up and then, what, then we're slaves to the system. Boom. No matter how free we say we are, we're still slaves. So I'm just making a point of it. I've lost faith in the system. You all can keep pretending, but I can't. And, call me crazy, but just maybe, the chains might contain the seeds of my liberation. Yeah, and when I do it, it won't be slavery like back in the day, what I'll go through will barely hold a candle to that horror-show, but, like the Buddha said, 'by putting up with the little cares, we train ourselves to bear the great adversity.'

MISHA. You snapped.

LEO. Yeah.

MISHA. Sounds like Afro-pessimism to the max.

RALPH (*reading*). The agreement is for 40 days.

MISHA. You don't want to be his slave for life?

LEO. 40 is an auspicious number. Jesus was 40 days in the desert, Hindus offer devotionals in groups of 40. The flood lasted 40 days and 40 nights. Buddha did 40 under the tree. 'Quarantine' comes from 'Quaranta' which means 40. Moses did 40 days on the mountain. The Prophet did 40 days in the cave. Jesus, again, did 40 when he fasted.

RALPH. 40 acres and a mule.

DAWN. Ali Baba and the 40 Thieves.

MISHA. 40 ounces of malt liquor.

LEO. In 40 days I'll have transcended it. Like the brother said 'Nothing can be changed until it's faced.' The pain and rage need to get worked out of my system. I'll take myself to the lowest place and know forever after that, if I can bear it, then I can bear anything. And my mind will be free.

RALPH. Who am I buying you from?

LEO. You're buying me from me.

RALPH. For how much?

LEO. Money's not the point.

RALPH. I gotta give you something. How about I give you 89 grand?

LEO. That'll be just enough to pay back my student loans.

RALPH. Bingo.

LEO. Meesh, could we come on your Show and talk about it?

MISHA. That would be called 'enabling.'

RALPH. Yeah, let's not.

DAWN (*reading*). 'I, Leo…, hereafter referred to as The Enslaved Person, agree to serve Ralph…, hereafter referred to as The Master, for an agreed-upon time…' It goes on.

LEO. It's what I want.

LEO *signs.* RALPH *picks up the pen but pauses.*

RALPH. I don't know if I want to do this I don't know if I'm comfortable with doing this I feel like my whole life, I mean,

my whole life up until this point I've been careful, no
mindful, I've been mindful because careful implies
somewhere in there a fear and I'm not afraid I'm just awake
I mean I'm just as awake as I can be given the facts of my
circumstances.

LEO. This isn't about you right now, ok?

RALPH. I'm a straight white guy and, while, theoretically,
I came from money, I grew up poor. Dirt poor and dirty and
bullied and shit on, metaphorically, I'm speaking
metaphorically about the dirt and the shit my mom always
made sure I was clean. Have you ever been washed by
someone who is afraid of what the kids and their parents will
think of you and of her if her kid showed up to school dirty?
My skin was always rubbed red. The water was always hot.
The soap was always strong. Her hands were always rough
and rubbing hard. Like she could wash my father, who was
already married to somebody else, and rich, and didn't give
a crap about us, like she could, just like the song, wash that
man right out of our hair and stop me from looking like him,
and somehow, the washing would make everything all right,
and we'd forget about the money that he had so much of and
that she needed and that we both needed but that never ever
came. And my teeth. Crooked and rotten cause I would sneak
candy after bedtime. When my dad found out that he was
dying, he sent his Help to locate me. Said he was dying. Said
he was leaving me a fortune. I did not cry in front of him.

LEO. Yeah, bro, you hate your dad. We know.

RALPH. I never told you this part. [They sent me car fare. This
was when I was back in high school, right, and I took the bus
down from Schenectady. All this time I'd been living in
Schenectady. He was sitting in a green leather easy chair. He
was wearing a designer sweatsuit, matching pants and jacket.
Fancy. Sitting there in the height of style. Shows me his
favorite memento: a photo of him and his dad shooting guns
with one of the Presidents. I forget which one. I didn't know
what to say. He stands up, he shakes my hand, and pulls me in
for a hug but I pull away and recoil so I can give him a fucking

left hook. And he smiles. And his smile stops my hand like
he's a super hero or some shit. 'Lemme have it,' he says.
I didn't do nothing. He bought me dinner. Two steaks I ate.
I did not cry on the way home. And when I did get home,
I just broke shit. The laptop, the dishes, my knickknacks.
Cause all I could think about was] When I was little, he would
come and visit me and Mom. And he would beat the shit out
of her. Literally. If you ever wonder what that means it really
means it. You can beat someone so hard that they shit
themselves. And I would cry. And she hated it when I cried but
I wanted to make things better and I didn't know what to do.
And this one time he hit her and scared her so bad and she was
afraid to get up so she just stayed where she was at, sitting on
the floor in the corner against the wall. The TV was on and she
was watching. Re-runs of <u>Laugh In</u> . And me crying and her
smoking her Virginia Slims. Letting the ash fall to the floor.
Whole house coulda burned down. 'Promise me you won't be
like him,' she says. And I said 'Yeah.' But the way I'm feeling
today – I don't know if I can keep that promise any more.

LEO. Stop talking. Stop.

RALPH. Right. It's time for the white guy to shut up. So yeah
maybe you're right. Yeah, like where do I sign?

LEO *takes in what* RALPH *just said. It gives him pause but
not enough to stop the train. He shows* RALPH *where to
sign.* RALPH *signs.*

LEO. And, at the end of the 40, when we've made it through,
we'll meet up here and have a party.

MISHA. Look at me, bro.

LEO. What?

MISHA. Like the brother said: 'The thoughtless drift backward
toward slavery.' I mean, do you really hate yourself that
much? You have got to love you.

LEO. I'm angry/

MISHA. /And you're taking it out on yourself. Like when we
riot, we burn down our own neighborhoods.

LEO. Yeah. Something like that.

DAWN. This is bad.

LEO. Shut up.

LEO
DAWN
(*Rest.*)

MISHA. You're mentally ill, made sick by the world we live in.

LEO. It'll be all right, K?

LEO
MISHA

MISHA. K.

>DAWN *looks over the signatures then, fishing in her bag, takes out her notary seal.*

RALPH. You walk around town with your notary seal?

DAWN. You never know. Misha, you're the witness.

MISHA. No way.

LEO. I'd do it for <u>you</u>.

MISHA. So?

RALPH. So do it for <u>me</u>, Meesh. If it helps Leo feel safe and work through/

MISHA. Fine./

LEO. Thanks./

>MISHA *signs. Then* DAWN *notarizes the document and hands it to* RALPH.

>RALPH *has set up a fresh paper target and yanked the pulley-rope to put the target in place.*

MISHA. You're both full of shit.

RALPH. Leo. Shoot.

ACT ONE, SCENE FOUR

LEO chooses a gun. Loads it. Zen-like as before. RALPH, as before, goes into his coach mode.

Focus. With your whole self. Become one with the target. Show them who <u>we</u> are. You hear me?!

LEO shoots. Another bullseye.

LEO. Yes!

They do their weird-athletic-bro-dance moves. They drink. They're hyped up and intoxicated.

MISHA. Stop it, guys.

DAWN. There is no stopping them.

LEO and RALPH are in their own world.

RALPH. But what am I going to tell people?

LEO. Tell them whatever you want.

LEO shoots again. With a lot more flair than before. Bullseye.

End of Act One.

ACT TWO

Scene One: Leo & Ralph (Day 1)

In RALPH *and* MISHA*'s apartment. The next morning.*

RALPH*'s shoes neatly shined.* RALPH*'s laundry cleaned and neatly folded. On a table:* LEO*'s sketchbook.* RALPH *in the bathroom.* LEO *nowhere in sight.*

We hear the toilet flush and then RALPH *enters. He's wearing his bathrobe. Phone in one hand and contract in the other, which he's perusing.*

As RALPH *enters from the restroom,* LEO *enters, coming from outside.*

RALPH. Good walk?

LEO. Very good.

   RALPH *gets a text. Glances at his phone.*

RALPH. Did you have a sign?

LEO. No. – . Yeah.

   LEO *removes the modest hand-written paper sign from his trouser pocket.* RALPH *grabs it.*

RALPH. 'I am the property of Ralph – ' We didn't say you could have a sign! What the fuck.

LEO. Don't worry. Nobody even noticed.

RALPH. Except the Dean. The head of my fucking department!

LEO. Oh. That's who that was.

RALPH. He lives around the corner!

LEO. I didn't know.
   (*Rest.*)

ACT TWO, SCENE ONE   61

I did your laundry, shined your shoes and then I went walking. Around your neighborhood. From 3 in the morning until now. Not one person bothered me. Not the cops. Nobody gave me a second look. Except this one guy. – Your Dean. He's jogging by 'he's in pretty good shape for an old white guy,' I'm thinking, and then he stops, jogs in reverse, looks me up and down. Takes a picture/

RALPH. /Picture, sends it to me. I'm texting back saying it's probably just some student joke. This is not good for me. I've got a brand. My students call me Righteous Ralph. And – I'm up for a promotion.

RALPH *texts*.

LEO. Sorry.

LEO *takes the sign. Balls it up. Tosses it out.*

RALPH. I'm asking Dawn and Meesh if they've told anybody else about your – Quest.

LEO. Ok.

RALPH *gets their responses.*

RALPH. Misha says 'Hell to the no.' Dawn wonders if we're calling it off.

LEO. Are we?

LEO
RALPH

LEO. I need this.

RALPH. I get that you need the protection but do we have to advertise it? I mean – right?

LEO
RALPH

LEO. How about if only the four of us know. It'll be internal. Which could still work. I guess. Except, if the cops –

RALPH. Understood.
(*Rest.*)

We'll have a gag rule.
(*Rest.*)
I'll put it in writing.

LEO. K.

RALPH *takes out his laptop and types.*

RALPH (*typing*). Amendment #1: 'During the 40-day period, and after the successful completion of said 40 days, both parties agree to non-disclosure. In all media.'

LEO. My lips are sealed.

RALPH. I'll ask the ladies to do the same.

LEO. Cool.

RALPH (*re: the contract*). I have to protect you, feed you, house you, and I get to tell you what to do.

LEO. Along the agreed-upon guidelines.

RALPH (*re: the contract*). You'll do the cleaning. Ok. I'll have the Cleaning Lady take a month off.

LEO. Plus 10 days. 40 days total.

RALPH. Didn't know you were such a stickler.

LEO. 40 days is 40 days.

RALPH. And could your chores include something like, I dunno, breaking someone's kneecaps or dumping what looks like a body bag into the river no questions asked?

LEO. Being your Enslaved Person does not put me above the law.

RALPH. Right.

LEO. Are you angry at someone, bro?

RALPH. I'm mad at the world but it comes and goes.

LEO. I hear that. I harbor a significant amount of confusion, disconnection and anger because of my Inherited Enslaved Persons' Trauma.

ACT TWO, SCENE ONE 63

RALPH. Is that even a real thing?

LEO. There's scientific research. Survivors of trauma develop <u>survival skills</u>. If said skills are practiced <u>outside</u> of the context of the <u>original</u> trauma, and then, <u>learned</u> by subsequent generations, one would find that, <u>sometimes</u>, those skills just might be more of a hindrance than a help.

RALPH. Sounds like you've been reading up on it.

LEO. Just staying up all night cleaning, thinking, walking.

RALPH. Could you make me some tea?

LEO. Sure.

>LEO *makes* RALPH*'s tea*.

I'm also aware that I have internalized a lot of Hate. I am aware that <u>Internalizing The Hatred</u> is a <u>survival skill</u>.

RALPH. You think?

LEO. Yep. And 'The only way out is through.' So, I'll purge myself. And then, I'll be truly free.

RALPH. And I'll be free too. Maybe I'll even start writing again.

LEO. Maybe. But don't/

RALPH. /Hope for too much, yeah.

>RALPH *notices* LEO*'s notebook*.

You were working. Drawing. And writing.

LEO. Last night. While you were sleeping.

RALPH. Good for you.
(*Reading from* LEO*'s notebook*.) 'Waking up is hard to do but staying woke is harder.' Deep shit.

LEO. Thanks.

RALPH. Amendment #2: For You: no reading, no writing.

LEO. Shit. Ok.

RALPH. Hand over your phone. And your wallet. [You can keep your driver's license.]

LEO *hands over what* RALPH's *requested.*

LEO. We're going deep.

RALPH. 'The only way out is through.'

LEO *serves the tea.* RALPH *drinks it.*

I didn't want green. I wanted black. Make me another pot.

LEO. Ok.

RALPH. Is this how you want me to be?

LEO. Is this how you want to be?

LEO
RALPH
(*Rest.*)

LEO *goes to make more tea.*

LEO. I laid out your clothes. You should get dressed. You've got your class to teach, and you're running late. You don't want your students missing out on their very valuable and very expensive education.

RALPH *heads into the bedroom to get dressed.* LEO *tidies up.*

RALPH *comes back into the living room holding his clothes: a shirt and tie, a tweed jacket and nice slacks.*

RALPH. I only wear these clothes when I visit my mother.

LEO. They're still trying to decide who's getting that job, right? That outfit is your winning move.

RALPH *goes back into the bedroom. The water boils.* LEO *makes more tea.*

And you should shower before you dress. You'll want to look and <u>smell</u> like a winner.

RALPH *comes out of the bedroom wearing something other than the clothes* LEO *laid out. Like a loud shirt and some short pants and some ratty sneakers.*

RALPH *sits and takes up the contract again.*

You're running late, Mister Ralph.

RALPH. 'Mister Ralph'? Nice touch. I'm gonna call you something new.

LEO. Like what?

RALPH. 'Thaddeus.'

LEO. Try it out.

LEO *walks around,* RALPH *calls out to him.*

RALPH. Thaddeus!? Thaddeus!!

LEO. WHO THE FUCK ARE YOU TALKING TO?!!

RALPH. Shit, man you almost made me pee myself.

LEO. Think about it. It's my first day on the plantation and you give me a new name and, what, I'm supposed to know who you're talking to? That's some shit.

RALPH. Right. We'll stick with Leo.

LEO. K.

RALPH (*continuing to read*). Says I'm not allowed to physically mistreat you. That kinda sounds like Slavery-Lite.

LEO. Yeah, I hear you.

RALPH. Another amendment?

LEO. Do it.

RALPH (*typing*). Don't worry, it's not like I'm going to send you to the hospital.

LEO. No worries here, Bro. I can take care of myself.

RALPH (*typing*). Of course you can. You work out more than me.

LEO. I do, bro.

RALPH (*more reading*). No forced sex.
   (*Rest.*)
   But what about <u>Droit Du Segneur</u>? 'The Rights of the Master'? It was a thing. Should we allow it?

LEO. You're full of shit.

RALPH types the additions. LEO looks over RALPH's shoulder trying to see what RALPH just added. RALPH shoos him away.

RALPH. Howbout no 'Bro' for the 40 days?

LEO. Ok.

They share a laugh as RALPH types.

RALPH (*continuing with the contract*). Do I get to claim ownership over any progeny that you create during this time?

LEO. Me and Dawn aren't preggers.

RALPH. But if somehow you guys do happen to get 'with child' can I have it? Although, it's not that I would want the kid. I hate kids.

LEO. So, would you sell it? That's not even funny.

RALPH. Right. It's just business.

RALPH types in those changes.

LEO. Is that all?

RALPH. For now. Printing.

RALPH prints the amendment. Directs LEO to take it out of the printer. LEO doesn't read it. Hands it to RALPH. RALPH signs then hands the pen to LEO.

Sign. With an X.

LEO signs with an X.

RALPH looks at the contract and the amendments. Then RALPH just stands there. Looking lost.

LEO. You're going to be way late for your class, Mr Ralph.

RALPH
RALPH

LEO. Mr Ralph?

RALPH. I didn't get the promotion.

LEO. Shit.

> RALPH *sits on the couch.* LEO *sits next to him.* RALPH *leans his head on* LEO*'s shoulder.*

RALPH. They said they needed Diversity. It's a real shame. Don't you think?

LEO. Yeah, Boss. It's a crying shame. Although – . Yeah, sometimes someone gets a job cause they're black. And sometimes – most of the time, someone gets a job cause they're white. Or someone gets a car loan at a better rate cause they're white. They don't get the job or the better loan because they're more qualified or because they have a better credit score. They don't get to buy the house in the nicer hood cause they're more accomplished. They get access to the nice things cause they're white. And we don't notice. We don't question their right to get the things they get. Say you got two people: a black girl, working as a coder in Silicon Valley and a white guy working as a point guard in the NBA. When you see the black girl you figure, 'yeah, she got that job cause of Affirmative Action,' but when you see that white guy you figure, 'he made the team cause he must be really really good!'

RALPH. So I should be ok about not getting the job.

LEO. When one door closes another door opens.

RALPH. True that.

> RALPH *is satisfied. He looks at the amendments, then hands the page to* LEO.

Hang this on the wall.

> LEO *gets some tape and does so.*

Feels good to be writing again. Yeah, the juices are flowing. Even if it's just – yeah. Feels good.

LEO. You should go to class regardless. Show them that, promotion or not, you are still standing. Be the Master that you truly are.

RALPH. No. Fuck them. I'm going to stay home and write.

LEO. That's a great idea, Mr Ralph.

RALPH. Yeah. This could be the best thing that's ever happened to me.

[*SLAVE-LABOR INTERLUDE: The days pass. The scenery changes. Then* **LEO** *takes out a vacuum cleaner and runs it over the floors, cleaning methodically.*]

Scene Two: Dawn & Misha (Day 7)

DAWN *and* LEO's *apartment. Morning.*

MISHA *doing her Show. Again, low-key camera, light, laptop and that red rotary phone. She's in the middle of talking with a caller who is finally getting around to asking their question.*

MISHA. Why is everything always about the men? Right. That's a good question, Tammy. Yeah, maybe cause we've been trained that way. Maybe cause they've been trained that way. And breaking free of the training takes work. One step forward, two steps back sometimes.

TAMMY FROM BOSEMAN. I hear that. We gotta do everything we can to dismantle the patriarchy.

ACT TWO, SCENE TWO 69

MISHA. Right on.

TAMMY FROM BOSEMAN. Peace out!

The call ends. As the phone rings with another caller –

MISHA. I'm grateful to everybody for joining us and especially grateful to all of you who are calling in. This is Misha on Day 7-in-a-Row of 'Ask A Black.' I've been showing up and representing 7 days in a row, yeah, for one whole week. Wondering if we would have the stamina for The Big Conversation, and yeah, seems like we can hang and keep the chat going, right? Like – like Mr Rogers says 'anything that's mentionable is manageable.' We've got time for a few more calls. Hi, who's this?

ROBERTA FROM PORTLAND. It's Roberta from Portland!

MISHA. Hey, Roberta! Welcome back!

ROBERTA FROM PORTLAND. 'Crabs in the bucket.' If it is a black thing, I would very much appreciate you explaining it to me, please.

MISHA. Right. Ok. 'Crabs in the bucket.' Is a phrase that's used to describe how – some members of the black community fail to assist each other in their upward progress, and actually, like crabs in a bucket, pull one another down as they attempt to rise up.

ROBERTA FROM PORTLAND. Excuse my language, but that's some fucked-up shit.

MISHA. Indeed it is.

ROBERTA FROM PORTLAND. Congrats on your 7 days in a row. Are you going to do 7 more?

MISHA. Don't tempt me.

The call ends. The phone rings again.

Last caller for today!

She picks up the phone. She's weary but enthusiastic.

TEDDY FROM PHILLY. I'm Teddy from Philly and I'll be quick cause your time is tight. I'm a culture critic and I want your take on 'Trauma Porn.' Why all the talk about slavery? What about black joy? I mean, I'm thinking let's have more focus on the wins, and less on the losses, right?

MISHA. You want Christianity without the crucifixion? Hey, when trauma stops happening, I'll stop talking about it.

TEDDY FROM PHILLY. Yeah, but – in the cosmic context – talking only encourages it.

MISHA. And in the mythic context the Shero visits hell in her effort to help save the people.

TEDDY FROM PHILLY. Ok, ok –

MISHA. Teddy, that's all the time we have today. But, tell you what, I'm gonna be back tomorrow and do 7 more days making a fierce 14! So we can all keep dealing with our shit! You all gonna keep calling in? You better! So, until tomorrow morning this is Misha saying keep it cool, keep it real, go for broke and please stay woke.

The Show comes to a close. MISHA*'s exhausted.* DAWN *comes out of the bedroom.*

DAWN. 7 more days? You're kidding, right?

MISHA. I'm not kidding. I'm processing. Purging. Pushing through. Leo's got his Quest and I've got mine. And mine's the better method if I may say so myself. But can you believe I quoted Mr Rodgers, 'Anything that's mentionable is manageable.'

DAWN. It's a good quote.

MISHA. From a dead white guy.

DAWN. It's still a good quote.

MISHA. I need better.
  (*Rest.*)
  Are you stressing? How many days until you and Frankie Jr go to court?

ACT TWO, SCENE TWO   71

DAWN. This time next week. Should be a quick trial. Fingers crossed.

MISHA. You've been prepping day and night. You feel good about it?

DAWN. How about a glass of wine?

MISHA. It's 9 in the morning.

DAWN. We'll put some orange juice in it.

MISHA
DAWN

MISHA. Cool.

DAWN pours large glasses of wine, gives each a splash of orange juice. They toast. Sip.

DAWN. You think we'll ever make it?

MISHA. Make it – ?

DAWN. You think Leo's right? What's the use of having faith in the system if you want to be a winner?

MISHA. If I'm not in the winner's circle I'm gonna be, at least, winner's-circle-adjacent.

DAWN. You and me both.

They drink.

MISHA. Thanks for letting me crash on your couch.

DAWN. You're welcome to stay for the whole 40 days.

MISHA. They're not going to last that long. Either Leo's going to quit or Ralph's going to quit.

DAWN. I should go over there and bring Leo back home.

MISHA. Don't. Cause they both have something to prove or something to work through. Which could mean that they're gonna be on their 'Slave Quest'/

DAWN. 'Slave Quest'!/

MISHA. / For the next 100 <u>years</u> which <u>could</u> mean that we might never see either of them ever again. Which would be sad cause they're like family but it wouldn't be the total end of the world.

Laughing, they toast to that. Then DAWN *starts coming unraveled.*

DAWN. My case is hard. It started out easy. It started out being really easy but now it's really hard.

MISHA. Can you talk about it?

DAWN. No. Lawyer–/

MISHA. /Client confidence./

DAWN. /Right.

MISHA *pours more drinks. More splashes of juice.* DAWN *works through her feelings.*

Why don't I just settle down and have kids? That's what the partners in the firm are thinking. Cause I'm never going to make partner there. And they all know it. 'That Dawn, she should just settle down and squeeze some out.'

MISHA. Remember what we said in college. That we would settle down but not settle for. How are we doing with that?

DAWN. Not great.
   (*Rest.*)
   I hate being woke. I hate it. I just want to go back to being asleep. I just wanna/

MISHA. /Go back to the olden days. Back when everybody knew their place. Women. POCs.

DAWN. I didn't mean it that way.

MISHA. No sweat.

DAWN
MISHA

DAWN. Leo asked me to marry him.

ACT TWO, SCENE TWO   73

MISHA. Wow.

DAWN. Yep. And I told him that I needed some time to think about it.

MISHA. Shit. He's a good guy.

DAWN. But now he's got his Quest thing.

MISHA. So wait and see how he does with it.

DAWN. It could be the magic cure-all.

MISHA. Probably not.

DAWN. Hey, you never know.

MISHA
DAWN

MISHA. Ralph didn't get that job.

DAWN. Shit. Did he deserve to get it? No. To his face I'd be like 'bummer.' I would tell him I feel bad, but I don't.

MISHA. He really wanted that job. But yeah, I hear what you're saying.

DAWN
MISHA

DAWN. How come you and me never became a Thing?

MISHA. Not for lack of trying.
(*Rest.*)
You put your hand up my dress and we kissed in the bathroom at McSorley's after we'd done all those tequila shots to celebrate the anniversary of Ralph's dad dying.

DAWN. You weren't wearing any panties.

MISHA. You weren't either.

They drink to that.

DAWN. You should have guests. On your Show. I could be one. It would help folks to know that some lawyers are good guys who will fight for them. Especially now that 'living while black' is being criminalized.

MISHA. Maybe could.

DAWN has another idea and another drink.

DAWN. Or your special guest could be a cab driver. This guy I met recently, I'll text you his info. Mamadou from Brooklyn by way of Nigeria. For some reason he wanted to explain to me why he doesn't like to give rides to black people.

MISHA. That's kind of a champagne problem, right? Having Leo on the Show would be icing-on-the-gravy but no fucking way that's going to happen.

DAWN. I know exactly what could help. Close your eyes and keep them closed.

MISHA closes her eyes. DAWN grabs some small index cards and starts scribbling on them.

MISHA. I could get more followers if I posted something scandalous.

DAWN. Don't peek.

MISHA. I say my Show's getting picked up but that's just me blowing smoke. Me getting real backers is a long shot. I mean like, who is really watching? Who is actually tuning in? Mostly black people? Mostly white? Asian folks? Folks from overseas? Millennials? Gen X? Boomers? I know black folks are watching but I wish more of them would call in. So we could have the real conversations. So we could get deep up into the real deal. Every time I get a 'like' I feel as if I sold something for it. How long until I sell out?

DAWN's finished scribbling. She's got about 5 cards.

DAWN. Open your eyes.

MISHA. We're going to play poker?

DAWN. How did Dawn ace the Bar Exam?

MISHA. Brilliant Miss Misha made lovely Miss Dawn some flashcards.

DAWN. So I just did the same for you. Sample Topics and Zinger Quotes.

DAWN's care energizes MISHA.

MISHA. How about I go 40 days in a row. 'Ask A Black, 40 Days In A Row, The Righteous Challenge.'

DAWN. That would be so great! Fuck yeah!

DAWN takes up a flashcard and reads from it.

On the Topic of Hair!
(*From a flashcard.*) Throw down a quote like 'Remove the kinks from your mind, not your hair.' Marcus Garvey.

MISHA. Or 'Black hair has magic, genius and power in it.' Angela Davis.

They high-five over that.

DAWN (*from a flashcard*). On the Topic of Perseverance: 'If you can't get rid of the family skeleton you may as well make it dance.' George Bernard Shaw.

MISHA. Or: 'I'm black and I'm proud.' James Brown.

DAWN. Ok, your quotes are better than mine.

MISHA. You're getting my juices flowing.

DAWN (*from a flashcard*). On the topic of Civic Responsibility. (*From a flashcard.*) Quote: 'I freed a thousand slaves/

MISHA *and* DAWN. /'and I could have freed a thousand more if only they had known that they were slaves.'

MISHA. Harriet Tubman.

DAWN. Frankie's guilty.
(*Rest.*)
He told me so. Last week. He had been saying he didn't kill the guy. But last week I go over to his house, his mom is sitting there listening, stone-faced, and he tells me that he did it. Killed the guy. Pulled the trigger. At first I pretended that I didn't hear him. So he said it again. Louder. Then I noticed that his mother was covering up her ears.

MISHA. Shit.
>   (*Rest.*)
>   Are you going to tell?

DAWN. Nope. I'm going to save him.

MISHA. Girl, that does not sound like a smart move. Leo goes nuts, Ralph goes nuts, now you? Don't let their shit pollute our shit.

DAWN. I am trying to save a kid from jail.

MISHA. You never lie. You're honest to a fault.

DAWN. It's only a White Lie.

MISHA. Told by a White Savior. I get why you would lie. You help him but you help you more. You want to play the game, but don't. Look at you. Wanting to be a guest on my Show. Making me flashcards.

DAWN. I am trying to help.

MISHA. I don't need you to save me, Dawn.

DAWN. I didn't say you did, Meesh.

MISHA. 'I hate being woke. I just wanna go back to sleep.' Well, some of us don't have that kind of luxury.

DAWN. Don't play the black card.

MISHA. That's the only card I got.

>   DAWN *throws the flashcards at* MISHA.
>
>   MISHA *gets her suitcase and quickly starts throwing her stuff in it.*

DAWN. You're going back to Ralph's?

MISHA. I'm going to my moms'.

DAWN. Take the cards.

MISHA. I appreciate you letting me stay here. I'll see you in a couple of weeks.

MISHA *is packed to go. As she nears the door –*

DAWN. Take the cards. Please take the cards.

MISHA *leaves the cards on the floor. Goes.* DAWN's *left alone.*

[*SLAVE-LABOR INTERLUDE: The days pass. The scenery changes. Then* **LEO** *enters with a dish pan that holds* **RALPH**'s *lovely teacups. He cleans one teacup neatly and thoroughly. Then he intentionally breaks the next cup. Perhaps looking around to see if he's been seen.*]

Scene Three: Leo & Ralph (Day 14)

In RALPH *and* MISHA's *apt. Around 12 noon. The Amendments, still taped to the wall.*

RALPH *has a new look: a 2-week old beard, plaid shirt buttoned to the chin, hair in a ponytail. He's looking like a happening hipster. He's recently come home. A shopping bag and a cardboard box by the door.*

'Your Love to Love Me' plays. LEO *dances and, as* RALPH *does his best to keep up,* LEO *encourages him.* LEO *is a pretty good dancer.* RALPH, *for all his efforts, is less so.*

LEO. Work it. Come on. You the man. You the Boss. Master. Sho-nuff. You know it. So show it. Mr Ralph. Shake that thing.

RALPH. I've gotten better, right?

LEO. In these past two weeks you have improved, yeah.

RALPH *turns the music off.*

RALPH. I got on the dance floor last night.

LEO. You finally got up the courage. Congrats, Mr Ralph. How'd it go?

RALPH. It felt very <u>Saturday Night Fever</u> cause I got over like a fat rat. From zero to hero. You shoulda seen me! I was really something. I'm almost sorry you weren't there.

LEO. That's our deal.

RALPH. Right.

LEO *notices the shopping bags and the box.*

LEO. You got the stuff?

RALPH. I did indeed. And there are some surprises.

LEO. Cool.

RALPH. I also got some compliments about my new look. It felt good.

LEO. And you stayed out all night. Sounds like you had a time.

RALPH. A good time was had by all.

LEO. Last night I had an amazing experience.

RALPH. Good. I'd like some breakfast.

LEO. A soufflé?

RALPH. Your soufflés are legendary.

LEO. Soufflé it is.

LEO *takes eggs and stuff out of the fridge.* RALPH *heads back into the bedroom.*

LEO *locates a cooking pan and turns on the oven.*

When RALPH *comes back, he's holding a wooden box. Out of the box, he removes an old pistol. A Luger.*

RALPH. My dad's gun. I always hated it. Until now.

LEO *smells the eggs and touches them to his face.* RALPH *studies his Luger.*

'Always treat the gun as if it's loaded.'

LEO. The eggs are a little old but they should work ok.

RALPH *begins cleaning the gun.*

RALPH. I watched my dad clean this once. It was like a holy ritual.

LEO. I thought you were going to let it rust away in that box.

RALPH. I'll polish it up. What the hell.

RALPH*'s cleaned guns before so he knows what he's doing. He points the gun to the ground to eject any rounds that might still be in the chamber.*

Meanwhile, LEO *is busy with the soufflé prep. He's good at it. He scrounges around finding more ingredients and piling them on the counter: butter that smells sweet, honey that tastes good, a fragrant very yellow lemon, a beautiful apple.*

We're going to have apples in it?

LEO. Yes, Mr Ralph.

LEO *cores and slices an apple.*

RALPH *first does a safety check. With the gun unloaded, he points it away from everything. Then, keeping his fingers away from the trigger guard,* RALPH *presses on the magazine clip to release the magazine.*

Our experiment. It's working. I think. I didn't want to talk about it too soon, but, after last night and, as of this morning, I'm sure. For the last two weeks I've been doing your chores, running your errands, taking walks at night – not wearing a sign – and still: cops haven't given me a second look. Once I started acting suspicious and this cop comes up to me wondering if I need directions. A couple of days ago a rich-looking lady makes eye contact and she smiles at me when I walk past her. And she doesn't clutch her purse. Store managers don't follow me around when I'm shopping. Cabs stop for me and take me wherever I want to go. Cause somehow they know that I'm yours. At first I thought it was just some bullshit coincidence or a few scattered random acts of civil <u>obedience</u>, right? But hey, maybe I'm giving off a 'slave vibe.' Or maybe it's just the power of positive thinking. Well, whatever it is, I'm feeling safe, protected and respected –

RALPH. It's just like with condoms.

LEO. How so?

RALPH. When you <u>don't</u> got your protection, that's when you need it.

LEO. Right.
(*Rest.*)
But, back to my point, Mr Ralph, the cherry on top, the smoking gun, if you will, the ultimate proof: Last night. I slept. The whole night through.

RALPH. No way.

LEO. I slept. A solid 8.

RALPH. Holy fuck.

LEO. Like a rock.

RALPH. Congratulations.

LEO. Gimme my phone I wanna text Dawn and tell her.

RALPH. No phone no contact.

LEO. You text her then, K?

RALPH. I understand you wanna give her the big news but, remember, man, it's early days. You've only got one good night under your belt. What if you slip up? Not saying you will, but –

LEO. But I could.

RALPH. Yeah. So tell her at the end of the 40. You'll be solid and she'll be like: wow!

LEO. Right.

LEO *melts the butter in the microwave.*

RALPH*'s still cleaning his gun.*

LEO *wipes the dish clean then lays the apples in the dish.*

RALPH. Have you ever cheated on Dawn?

LEO. Nope. Never.

LEO *separates the yolks from the whites.*

RALPH. I cheated on Misha. Last night. I never have before. Never ever. I'm always trying to be good. But last night I slipped.

RALPH *looks into the chamber, making sure all the bullets are removed. He sticks his pinky finger into the chamber to make double sure that the chamber is empty.*

LEO. You want lemon zest?

RALPH. Sounds great.

LEO *grates the lemon.*

LEO *continues with his soufflé-making. He adds honey and lemon juice to the butter.*

RALPH *continues with his gun-cleaning. He pushes the slide forward and slips it off the receiver. He removes the recoil. He holds the barrel by the bottom lug and pulls it out of the slide. He lays out his cleaning tools: bore brush, gun-cleaner, toothbrush, a cloth.*

He cleans the barrel with the bore brush. He dabs gun-cleaner on the toothbrush then cleans the lug area. He wipes it all down with a cloth.

LEO *continues making the soufflé.* RALPH *puts his gun back together.*

I've been doing research. Back in the day, to train a slave, the most effective methods were psychological. Make your slave hate you. Which will somehow intensify his love for you. 'Seasoning,' they'd call it.

RALPH *has reassembled his gun, returned it to the box, locked the box and returned the box to the bedroom.*

Back in the living room, RALPH *eyes* LEO*'s notebook. He turns the pages.*

You're drawing a lot.

LEO. Yeah, well. In between the chores.

RALPH. I love the new stuff.

LEO. Thanks.

> RALPH *tears out the pages from* LEO's *notebook and pockets them.*

RALPH. Mine.

LEO. You're kidding.

RALPH. I'm not.

LEO. Right. Ok. A little privilege goes a long way.

RALPH. What?

LEO. Nothing.

> LEO *beats the yolks. Then he beats the whites.*
>
> (*Rest.*)
> Miss Malvina, she would say, whipping the eggs allows the molecules to bond more effectively.

RALPH. She was your science teacher, right?

LEO. She taught Science <u>and</u> Home Ec.
 (*Rest.*)
 This should be ready in a little bit.

> LEO *pours it in the pan and puts it in the oven. Sets the oven timer.*

RALPH. Great. Can't wait. Let's check out the bags.

> LEO *takes up a bag. Looks into it. He takes out a new black cotton T-shirt. Looking it over, then putting it on over what he's already wearing. The T-shirt says 'Slave.'*

LEO. This is a bold choice.

RALPH. It's only for you to wear around the house. Put what's in the box on my desk.

> LEO *does so. It's a manual typewriter.*

You feel like meeting a few of my new friends?

ACT TWO, SCENE THREE 83

LEO. You made new friends? Do they know about my Quest?

RALPH. Not at all. They're business guys. Deep Pockets. From the bar. Stupid-Rich. They'd love to meet you. It'd be good for your career and our Quest stays on the Q-T.

LEO. So, let's meet them. Cool. Can do.

RALPH. Now go out in the hall.

LEO goes.

We were talking shackles.

LEO. Right.

RALPH. But, I researched it and I think I did better.

LEO comes back in holding a large iron slavery-collar.

LEO. It's a punishment collar.

RALPH. It's from a museum. More like a private collection. A loaner. Let's put it on.

LEO. Looks like it'll break my neck.

RALPH. It's pretty safe if you're just standing still. I talked to the head curator. Apparently it's only dangerous if you're running. Like through the woods. Those little barb things catch on branches and would make you trip and you wouldn't be able to stop your own fall and then your neck would snap in two. And then there's the sheer weight of it just on its own. It's tricky to balance. The strings I had to pull to get the guy to lend it to me. And the looks I got trying to get it into a cab. But yeah, I can tell what you're thinking. No way do you want to put that on. It's a punishment collar and you haven't misbehaved. I hear you. Put it on anyway. The only way out is through, right?

LEO
RALPH

RALPH. I'll spot you.

LEO. Cool.

RALPH helps LEO put on the slavery-collar. It's unwieldy and dangerous and horrible.

If you think about it, in the enslavement of people, and in the 'discovery' and conquering of lands, there was a lot of rape, forced sex for breeding, and probably a whole lot of kinked-up sexual tension.

RALPH. Probably. It looks heavy. How does it feel?

LEO. Heavy.

RALPH. Could you get up/

LEO. /On the table?

RALPH. /Table? I'll help.

LEO. /Yeah sure.

With RALPH*'s help,* LEO *gets up on the table.*

RALPH. Just stand still. Don't hurt yourself.

LEO *just stands there.*

RALPH *stands back regarding the tableau: A black man dressed in a 'Slave' T-shirt wearing an iron slavery-collar.*

LEO. How bout we go to the range? Shoot some guns, blow off some steam?

RALPH. I closed the place. For renovations.

LEO. It was great like it was.

RALPH. I want it to have a whole new vibe.
(*Rest.*)
I'm getting in touch with my heritage. Thanks to you. Your Quest has inspired me.

LEO. Glad to be of service.

RALPH
LEO
RALPH
LEO

RALPH *goes to his desk. Puts paper in the typewriter.*

LEO, *still standing there, 'Slave' T-shirt and slavery-collar around his neck.*

LEO. Let's take the collar off now, right?

LEO
RALPH

LEO. Right?

> RALPH *does not answer. But he does begin typing.*
>
> *The oven timer sounds.*

Scene Four: Misha's Solo (Day 21)

MISHA. I'm 21 Days in with my Show and I don't know if I can keep doing it. Everybody's calling. Asking me their questions. It's a trip, cause I'm up here at my moms'. So, while I'm reaching out to the whole world I'm also up here in my old stomping grounds, going down memory lane. I'm expanding and contracting. The whole world gets to call me, but who do I get to talk to?
(*Rest.*)
I'm one of the lucky ones. 2-parent family. 2 moms, BTW. Both of them professors, Afro-Am-Studies and Women's, well, Gender Studies. Both of them very loving, very kind. Both of them very black. Not in terms of skin tone necessarily, but in terms of mindset. In terms of level of pride. In terms of level of consciousness. Righteousness. Sometimes self-righteousness. The town, a college town, where I grew up is very progressive, very welcoming. There was that one time when my 5th-grade class was studying slavery and I was only black kid in the room and so all the kids' eyes were on me. Looking. Asking. My moms say that my upbringing wasn't the typical black experience. And that in itself could be some boon or some baggage. I was always getting straight As, then I double majored, History and Philosophy, and graduated at the top of my class, so my moms expect a lot of me. I tell them I'm finding my way just fine. Cause I got my Show.
(*Rest.*)

'Hey this is Misha, welcome to "Ask A Black"' yeah, on my
Show I play black. I dial up the ebonics, employ the gestures
and linguistic characteristics most often featured in
Communities of African Descent. On my Show I perform my
blackness, cause I feel like, if I don't act black, then folks
looking for the real deal won't call in. Cause they won't see me
as authentic. Whatever that means. And what is 'acting black'
anyway? And why does 'acting black' only mean a certain
thing, and usually not a good thing? These days, in some
contexts, <u>acting</u> black, is marketable, and in other contexts, it's
not. <u>My moms do not know what to think of my Show.</u> I'm
trying to get them on as guests. They're still on the fence. They
say 'You are the ambassador of your race and, when you do
something stupid, your behavior sets us all back 100 years.'
Yeah, but it's more complicated than that. Cause, these days,
it's hard to distinguish what is <u>stupid</u> from what is stupid-
<u>necessary</u>. Cause, maybe the Movement don't move the old
way no more. Cause maybe acting black is what folks <u>want</u> to
see. And not just white folks. If we could place the blame for
all the shit on the shoulders of the white folks, then we would
be on easy street, right? Hey, the macro- and microaggressions
that people like ME do to people who LOOK LIKE me – that
shit has got to stop! But, don't get me wrong: Fact Number
One: White Folks gotta take responsibility for their bullshit.
And then there's Fact Number 2: So do We. There I go again,
standing on my soapbox. I used to come home after work and
I'd stand in the living room and go off. When I told Ralph that
I needed a soapbox, he went and brought me an actual
soapbox. Thanks, but what I really needed was to be heard and
seen. And I started my Show from there.
(*Rest.*)
Racism is a virus. And we've all got it. Ok, some more than
others, ok. The <u>workings</u> of the virus are getting more
complicated and the <u>rewards</u> are getting more sophisticated.
And Black folks should be supporting each other lock-step,
cept we don't. Cause cutting each other down is what we were
taught and what we seem happy to perpetuate. Crabs in a
bucket. And why is that? And how do we divest ourselves
from the negative implications that culture has attached to the

Negro when negative and negro, N-E-G, are connected at the root? Go beneath the root. And how the hell are we supposed to do that?
Maybe those are the things that Leo is gonna figure out. Even though he's always been a little broken, my moms, they love Leo. They like Dawn. And yeah, they do not like Ralph. They want me to dump him. It's not a racist thing. It's just that, whenever I talk about Ralph they just go quiet.
(*Rest.*)
There's White Noise, there's Pink Noise, and there's Black Noise. White noise puts you to sleep, pink noise is healing, and black noise is silence.
(*Rest.*)
And we got stuff like White Guilt: good people feeling bad for things that are not directly their fault. But there's also Black Guilt. Like when one appears to look guilty even when you're just walking around minding your own business. And so when we pass the cops on the street we smile a lot, or we look down at the sidewalk.
(*Rest.*)
Did you ever set out to go somewhere and you ended up somewhere else? That, in a nutshell, is one of the cornerstones of the African Diaspora. Lost. Lost. Lost. The whole world, it's a big can of worms. Something is decomposing and worms are feeding on it. Yeah. Some folks are doing their best to make things right, but to really fix the shit, you gotta go all the way back. Back through the portal of history, back through the rabbit hole, the abyss, the void, back through the wormhole, yeah, the wormhole as wide as the world.
(*Rest.*)
Everybody's calling me. Cept Leo. He hasn't called yet. And he's the only one that I really wanna talk to. Cause, other than that, I'm sick of talking with people. Blacksplaining the world is working my last nerve. Shouldn't we have all the answers already? But we don't. Yeah.
(*Rest.*)
21 days in a row and 19 more to go. Yeah, that's right. Keep Calm and Black On.

[SLAVE-LABOR INTERLUDE: The days pass. The scenery changes. LEO enters with RALPH's typewriter. He changes the ribbon. Gets ink on his hands.]

Scene Five: Dawn and Ralph (Day 28)

At the Spot. Late night. The place is in the process of being renovated. We can see some of the results. A fresh coat of paint in progress, ladders, buckets, brushes in evidence. Other elements still under wraps: colorful furniture, cute lighting, a karaoke machine. Keeping with the no-alcohol safety vibe, the bar would only sell soft drinks and food. There's a photobooth, family-friendly signage.

RALPH, *using his father's Luger, repeatedly aims and fires at the targets. He's got style and he's a great shot.* DAWN, *dressed in a cute outfit, watches.*

RALPH (*as he hits his marks*). Yes. Yes. Yes. Yes.

DAWN. You're better than you were in college.

RALPH. Watch and learn.

>RALPH *presses a button on his phone, activating the target-retrieval systems.* DAWN *is impressed.*

The target-retrieval system is now totally automated.

DAWN. You really are having the whole place redone.

RALPH. I'm taking a chance. On myself.

DAWN. We gotta drink to that! I brought us some Minis.

>*While* RALPH *changes the paper target,* DAWN *digs in her purse, pulling out several mini-bar-size bottles of bourbon, gin and vodka.*

RALPH. It's like old times.

ACT TWO, SCENE FIVE   89

DAWN. Memory Lane here we come.

They choose their bottles and open them. RALPH *barely sips his,* DAWN *gulps hers down.*

Thanks for the lesson.

RALPH. Thanks for asking.

DAWN. How else was I gonna get you to hang out? Our weekly Thing at the Spot is on hiatus. I'm guessing cause you don't let your Enslaved Person handle firearms.

RALPH. That is correct. Plus it's giving me a chance to update the place. We'll re-open again after the Quest.

DAWN. I miss this place.

RALPH. Really?

DAWN. Distance makes the heart grow. Ok. My turn.

RALPH. Take your pick.

RALPH *gestures to the gun table.* DAWN *examines the guns.*

DAWN. Some of these are really pretty.

RALPH. It's all part of the inclusive ambiance.

DAWN *chooses a pink Glock and a magazine of bullets, puts on her ear and eye safety gear. She's about to load the gun then –*

Ceasefire!

DAWN. What did I do wrong?

RALPH. I smell alcohol on your breath.

DAWN. I only had the one. Ok, so I went for drinks before I came here.

RALPH. 'On the Range we only drink in moderation.'

DAWN. Don't be such a tight-ass. You were always, underneath that bad-boy behavior, you were always such a tight-ass.

RALPH. Safety first.

DAWN *partially removes her eyes and ears (safety gear).*

DAWN. You want more kudos?

RALPH. Not at all.

DAWN. You want more kudos. I can tell. Always could.

RALPH. Ok gimme more kudos.

DAWN *compliments* RALPH. *She makes it feel like the first time.*

DAWN. Oh, Ralph! The place is gorgeous! You – you redoing everything! Look at the furniture! Look at the lights! Oh, they're so cute! And the – karaoke!?! Shit! And a photobooth just like the one in McSorley's! How many photos did we take in there, right? People will want to hang out here, Ralph! I mean, people already do, serious shooters will appreciate the equipment upgrades but, now you can also have birthday parties, bachelorette parties, sweet 16s, bar and bat and b'nai mitzvahs! Gender-reveal parties! Quinceañeras, Kwanzaa Nights!

RALPH. I'm also thinking merch, giftcards.

DAWN. So inclusive! So welcoming! So Fun! Kudos!

She's genuinely celebrating him and he's totally enjoying it. They're overcome with laughter. She opens another Mini. Downs it. He's still on his first one.

RALPH. Me and Leo, we're going deep. 28 days in.

DAWN. And 12 days to go.

RALPH. Leo is really coming to grips, you know?

DAWN. With what?

RALPH. His shit. You know, his <u>black</u> shit.

DAWN. Ok. But is he ok?

RALPH. He's great. He's painting again. I'm having him repaint the place.

ACT TWO, SCENE FIVE   91

DAWN. That's weird, Ralph.

RALPH. Maybe, but he says he's feeling more at home in the world. And he's sleeping through the night.

DAWN. Wow. No way.

RALPH. Every night since Day 14. Technically it started the night of Day 13.

DAWN. So he's better?

RALPH. He's doing great. And I keep him busy.

DAWN. Well, that was the deal.

RALPH. I didn't get that job, though.

DAWN. Oh. Bummer.

RALPH. But I'm writing again.

DAWN. No shit.

RALPH. Yeah.

DAWN. Cheers. Good for you.

They drink. DAWN *starts another Mini.* RALPH *is still on his first.*

RALPH. I'm writing about stuff from childhood.

DAWN. Heavy.

RALPH. And one of my new pieces is getting published.

DAWN. Holy shit, Ralph. Cheers.

They drink.

RALPH. It's all coming together.

DAWN. You want to get in my pants, don't you?

RALPH. I – uh, no I don't.

DAWN. You're writing. About childhood. And you're getting published. Those were the things I was always nagging you about.

RALPH. I feel like I've got more focus these days.

DAWN. That Master-Slave thing is really working for you.

RALPH. I guess.

DAWN
RALPH

They drink.

DAWN. You. Are. Getting. *Published*.

They drink.

RALPH. You and Meesh aren't getting along?

DAWN. Meesh, she's just always right all the time which means I'm always wrong.

RALPH. Yeah, I've been there.

DAWN. I guess I was getting in the way of her vibe.

RALPH. Her Show is getting intense. I've been watching. When she had her moms on. And did you see the one with that Cab Driver?

DAWN. I haven't been watching. I've been busy. And I've been celebrating. My case.

RALPH. Yeah! I've been so wrapped up in my own shit! Hey! Congrats to you! I coulda sworn your guy was guilty but he just sailed through the whole thing unscathed.

DAWN. I'm good at what I do.

RALPH. And you do it good too.

DAWN
RALPH

RALPH. Just paying you a compliment.
   (*Rest.*)
   Congratulations on your case. You're a Superstar.

   DAWN *takes* RALPH*'s Mini. Finishes it for him. They laugh.*

Ok. We'll practice. But only dry-fire.

DAWN. No ammo?

RALPH. Nope.

DAWN relinquishes her magazine of ammo. Satisfied that they're safe, RALPH goes into coach mode.

Stand on the line, Superstar. Just pretend the gun is loaded.

DAWN, wearing her eyes and ears, and holding her unloaded gun, stands on the line. RALPH comes to stand behind her, touching her a little. She very methodically takes her stance, aims down-range.

Your grip is good. Finger off the trigger until you're lined up. Widen up your stance a little. Line up your sights. Front-sight-back-sight. Fire.

DAWN fires the gun. As it's not loaded, all we hear is the click.

DAWN. My aim always pulls to the right.

RALPH. You wanna use just the tip of your fingerpad and squeeze it off gently.

She tries again.

DAWN. Better, right?

RALPH. Yeah, but your breathing is all wrong, Inhale. Exhale. Hold. Shoot.

DAWN takes another try with the breathing.

DAWN. Inhale. Exhale. Hold.

RALPH. You ever cheated on Leo?

DAWN. No.

DAWN shoots several times. Again, as it's only dry-fire, we only hear the clicks.

RALPH. You're getting the hang of it.

DAWN. Thanks. I've been getting offers from other law firms. Good ones. They're calling me saying that they'd like me to consider joining their team.

RALPH. Cause you're a Superstar.

DAWN. Cause they think I'm one of the good guys.

RALPH
DAWN
RALPH
DAWN

They start kissing. It turns into sex. It starts out hot then it gets clumsy. Especially with the gun-safety eyes and ears. RALPH *has a condom. He's prepared. It's frantic. Then awkward. Then quick. They both cum, so it's good, but it's also kind of bad/sad. They've been here before. They collapse into giggles.*

DAWN. Can I read it? Your –/

RALPH. /Short story. When it comes out. /

DAWN. /Which?/

RALPH. /The New Yorker/

DAWN. Shit, Ralph. Boom.

They fist-bump. DAWN *finishes her Mini.*

RALPH. It was totally merit-based, but yeah, I did pull some major strings to fast-track it.
(*Rest.*)
I feel like I'm finally going to make something of myself.

DAWN. It's your time.

RALPH. You think?

DAWN. Things are coming together for you.

RALPH. And for you too, right?

DAWN. Totally.

RALPH. Cheers.

They drink. DAWN *lots.* RALPH *less.*

ACT TWO, SCENE FIVE 95

I met up with my Dean. It was a couple of days after Leo had started his Quest. Out of the blue, pretty much, the Dean wants to go for coffee. He'd been really supportive through the whole job thing.

DAWN. It's good to have him on your side.

RALPH. We talked. It was nice. He understands what I'm feeling. Says it's unfair. Says I'm next in line so that's cool. Then he looks around to make sure no one is watching and he hands me this very nice white business card.

RALPH *takes a business card from his pocket. Shows it to her.*

DAWN. It's totally blank. Nice paper, though.

RALPH. He tells me to take a selfie with it and post it online so whoever follows me would see it.

DAWN. I saw it. Wondered what it was. Felt kinda creepy.

RALPH. Within 10 minutes, of me posting. I get a message with an address and a date and a time. I was being invited to something so I went.

DAWN. You're kidding.

RALPH. It was in a nice apartment. Doorman building.

DAWN *has another Mini.*

DAWN. What part of town?

RALPH. Whatever.

DAWN. Who was there?

RALPH. Some guys. Just some guys. Just. A bunch of white guys.
(*Rest.*)
'White Club' they call it.

DAWN. Shit. 'White Club'?

RALPH. At first I thought it was a joke. But I didn't laugh. Which was a good thing.

DAWN. And you walked out of there as fast as you could.

RALPH. Pretty much.
   (*Rest.*)
   It was a weird scene. The Club. All they did was stand in a circle. Some people sat. And they shared. Stories.

DAWN. 'White Club.'

RALPH. I got out of there as fast as I could.

DAWN. Good for you. Shit. You're not going back.

RALPH. Of course not. I promise. Geeze.

She takes more mini bottles out of her purse. Lines them up. Drinks them down as he watches.

DAWN. I feel bad.

RALPH. You're too honest for your own good.

RALPH *tidies up, tossing out the condom, putting away the guns, safety gear and ammo. Gathering up the mini bottles.*

DAWN
DAWN

RALPH. Do you recycle these?

DAWN *pulls herself together as best she can.*

[*SLAVE-LABOR INTERLUDE: The days pass. The scenery changes.* **LEO** *enters with* **RALPH***'s dirty laundry. He dutifully separates the whites from the coloreds.*]

Scene Six: Dawn's Solo (Day 29)

DAWN. I'm not really here. I mean, that's what I wish now. That I were somewhere else. Far away. Where probably the same shit in some form or another is going on but it wouldn't have anything directly completely directly to do with me. So I could feel better. Just a little more ok. Cause all I feel right now is bad. I'm one of the good guys. I've always been one of the good guys. Tried to be. Ever since 4th grade in Mrs Barnwell's class when this girl named Lisa had a lazy eye and got teased by the boys and I stood up for her at recess I got sand poured on my head and everybody laughed at me and I felt bad but at least I did something. Everybody else was just standing there watching the injustice happen. And I helped. Or tried to. And everybody laughed at me. Even lazy-eye Lisa. What the fuck. Still, to this day, for the most part, I'm a do-gooder. And, right now, I feel bad. I asked Ralph to meet me at the Spot so that I could – I dunno. Just have some company. Him and me in college were two skanky teenagers. He was truly skanky and I was a skank-wannabe. He had grown up poor and then came into money and I had grown up with things. All the things that a kid can have when both her parents are psychiatrists. Both of them. And me their only child. I had things. That other kids didn't have. And I felt – and I feel – moved to – help. And people hate on me for that. And I feel bad.

(*Rest.*)

We're suspicious of do-gooders. How come?

(*Rest.*)

My parents, they did a great job raising me. They were always regular. As if they always had a piece of string between them and they always kept it pulled taut and even. I've never seen or heard them fighting. I've also never seen or heard them being affectionate. When I passed the Bar Exam they wanted me to accept the offers from the prestigious firms where my good works would have the greatest impact. They were bummed that I chose to work where I do. They were glad when I broke up with Ralph. They are thrilled about me and Leo. For all the wrong reasons. I catch them looking at us together, last year, at their annual Labor Day cookout. We're sitting together and I catch them looking at us and I see them smiling. Like my love for Leo is part of some social-justice project. And that, in turn, makes them better people. And I should call them on it. And I feel bad. That I don't – shit, if I called them on it, that would mean violating the Contract we have. The Contract that I have with my parents. A contract that I've agreed to carry out except that I don't exactly know the terms. What are the Rules? They're not written down anywhere. They're not spoken. But they're known. And they surface. And if the Contract were written down it would say something like 'we have agreed to be Do-Gooders so that we don't have to deal with who we really are.' Geeze. Yeah, nobody is to blame and everybody is complicit.

(*Rest.*)

I should be on top of the world. I should be throwing a party cause Frankie Junior got off scot-free. The kid totally kept his head down and the buck got passed to the kids who were already on their way to the shithole. But Frankie, I saved him because I was determined to save somebody. Because we don't need another black kid in jail. I said to myself, I'll be damned if I can't at least save one fucking person. And I was almost about to give up. Cause the firm I work for is shitty. When I started I was green and ready to learn and I thought I could turn them around, show them the light, help them embrace the angels of their fucking better natures but no. They kept me at the bottom. I've been some kind of joke to them. They call me The Saint. Cause I work with all the hopeless cases. The second offenders, the third offenders. The one's deemed lost, deemed not worth saving. And I was in the habit of holding the kids' hands, speaking metaphorically of course, holding their lost hands while they travelled from one shitty institution to the next and I couldn't ever seem to do anything to save even one of them. And I was getting in the habit of that. I was getting in the habit of losing. And I wanted to win, ok? And then, they assigned me Frankie. And I knew he was not innocent. Yeah, right from fucking jump. But I so wanted him to be. For once I would defend a winner. Frankie was charming and he lied to me and I knew he was lying and I didn't – yeah – I didn't care. And then, yeah, he <u>told</u> me he had a little hand in it. Actually a big hand in it. And my only thought was that I wish the little turd had kept the truth to himself. Cause I knew he was guilty right from the jump. And I didn't give a shit. And all my powers to rescue and save, all my superpowers came into play and so he will not do the time for a crime he did actually commit and I feel bad but then I tell myself that I've done a good thing. And I tell myself that shit like this happens every day.

(*Rest.*)

I feel bad. And I'm sinking. Sinking down.

(*Rest.*)

If you've got friends, real friends, of different – I'll just say it, friends of different colors or persuasions or ethnic groups or whatever, I mean, to have friends, real friends who are different from who you are, if you've got a friend like that, then you should get a fucking trophy. And realize that, in their absence, you are not who you are when you are in their presence. Their friendship sustains your better nature. And without their presence, you would fall back into your old habits. Which is, at the end of the day, why I think we need each other.

(*Rest.*)

Misha wants to stick with Ralph. And Ralph. Geeze. We reverted to our skanky-kids behavior which I gotta believe does not exist in either of us separately but only gets summoned up when we are alone together and I am drunk and he is – angry. And White Club. Geeze. And me and Leo. He's really trying. So what's up with me? I spend my days helping total strangers but I can't even help the guy I love. Cause the Contract is broken, people. That contract, that Social Contract that nobody seems to remember having signed. Which is why common courtesy seems more and more like a fucking miracle. Which is why everything that feels so sure, can so easily fall apart. And then what? And then we'll just keep on going somehow, maybe. And when Leo gets done with his Quest, we'll just, you know, have a party and pretend to pick up the pieces. Cause that's what we do.

Scene Seven: Misha and Leo (Day 35)

In MISHA *and* RALPH*'s apartment. Amendments still on the wall.*

LEO *still wearing his 'slavery T-shirt.'*

And he's a guest on MISHA*'s Show.* MISHA *has arranged her low-tech set-up. We catch* LEO *mid-conversation with a caller who seems friendly enough.*

BOB FROM DETROIT. Simple question. What exactly are you doing, man?

LEO. Like I was starting to tell The Caller before: In terms of the day-to-day: chores. The usual. My Master likes to watch me step and fetch. He had me wearing a collar. It got me thinking about all the brothers and sisters who have gone through the pain. And their hurt and their rage and how we're still carrying it around today. On our necks. On our backs. In our hearts. At first, we agreed to keep my Quest private. Then he went and took it public. Just last night, he took me to meet some of his friends and all I'll say about it is that I was exposed to some seriously disturbing bullshit. It was relatively mild from a historical perspective but he totally stepped over the line. Upside of the downside is that now I'm going public too, by talking with all of you. I'm figuring things out. I'm shedding some light on the modern-day predicament. I was standing in the crosshairs. Now I'm standing at the crossroads. I don't got none of answers but I do got some of the questions. So yeah, let's have the conversation.

BOB FROM DETROIT. I appreciate the rhetoric, but enslaving yourself of your own free will? That's a slap in the face to everything our people have gone through. You're just some college-educated kid who's playing a game that completely dishonors the actual Experience.

MISHA. Bob from Detroit, let's remember that Leo is engaging in a courageous 40-day experiment. 35 days so far with only 5 days to go.

BOB FROM DETROIT. What's courageous about it? There's no danger for him. So things are getting uncomfortable and now he's complaining. With his actions, he's saying that 'slavery is great.'

LEO. I'm not saying great things about slavery. I'm saying horrible things about the world.

BOB FROM DETROIT. Whatever you're saying, I'm saying shame on you for doing it and shame on her for giving you a platform. The whole thing is an entitled and ridiculous stunt.

The line goes dead.

MISHA. Ok, we're out of time for today but, hey, we're going to be back with you tomorrow and for the rest of the week as we complete our 40-days-in-a-row Righteous Challenge. This is Misha with Leo as today's special guest on 'Ask A Black' saying keep it cool and keep it real, go for broke and please stay woke.

MISHA *turns off the livestream technology.*

You good?

LEO. I'm all right. Thanks for coming right away. It wasn't easy finding a payphone.

MISHA. Did it help? Getting on the Show? You really spilled it.

LEO. The Slave done broke the Massa's rules. Mister Ralph's free to do what he wants, but not me. And what's he going to do when he finds out?

MISHA. Maybe it's time to stop the Quest.

LEO. I broke the rules, so now he's in his rights to break me.

MISHA. But you guys have an agreement.

LEO. That doesn't mean anything any more. But shit, if he tries something on me I'll stand up to him. There's a whole tradition of enslaved people who stood up and fought back.

MISHA. Quit, man.

LEO. And let him say that he won? I'm going to finish this.

MISHA
LEO

MISHA. Tell me more about Ralph's new friends.

LEO. They're just a bunch of white guys. That's all.

LEO
LEO

LEO. How are your moms?

MISHA. They're good. And they sent you a present.

She digs in her bag.

This episode of Black Joy is being brought to you by:

From her bag she takes a nice-sized spliff.

LEO. Oh, yeah! When I called you I didn't want to say it over the phone so I was using my/

MISHA & LEO. Negro Telepathy/

LEO. /Like, 'Please Misha please bring me some of the weed from your moms' summer garden!'

MISHA. Grade-A, and pre-rolled for your immediate enjoyment. Misha and her moms do not disappoint!

LEO. High-Five To My Higher Power!

They high-five the sky.

MISHA *lights it and they smoke.*

Awesome sauce like Diana Ross! Cotton-doogly-woogly!

MISHA. You are so colored.

LEO. Look who's talking.

They pass the spliff back and forth.

MISHA. It's a great time to be black, right?

LEO. – . Yeah. But woke takes work.

More smoking. More smoking.

I ever tell you about my great-grandma on my mother's side? Built sidewalks in West Texas. Owned a hair salon and a barber shop.

MISHA. How about your grandfolks before that?

LEO. Can't trace them. Records burned. Folks killed. No clue who they were.

MISHA. Same here. I used to get jealous of the folks who can trace their families way back. Must feel good to know your people.

LEO. Word.
(*Rest.*)
Do you think Dawn still loves me?

MISHA. I dunno. You should ask her.
(*Rest.*)
She's got a new job. She's been posting about it.

LEO. Oh.

MISHA. When does Ralph get home?

LEO. No comment.

MISHA
LEO

MISHA *takes a big drag from the spliff.*

MISHA. As God is my witness, Ralph is my weakness.

LEO. You never fell for me that way.

MISHA. Sure I did. You just never felt it. You're head over heels with Dawn but you weren't ever like that with me.

LEO. Cause she let me be like that. Maybe I took you for granted. But with you, you were always holding a mirror up to me and I was always falling short.

MISHA. And with you I felt respected – but not protected.

LEO. Remember you and me in the back of my Ford Fiesta?

MISHA. It was my first time.

LEO. Mine too.
   (*Rest.*)
   Black Love.

MISHA. Too bad we didn't make it.

MISHA
LEO

LEO. I've started feeling my feelings instead of just thinking I'm feeling my feelings. I've been feeling all kinds of shit, like, I dunno. The Time before Time was even invented. And then: The Dawn of Time itself. The Gravity of The Mother Continent. The Parade of History. The Daily Tide of Systemic Racist Bullshit. The Calculus of Injustice. The Reality of Inherited Trauma. The Fragility of The Man Behind The Curtain. I'm seeing shit that I can't unsee. I'm feeling shit that I can't unfeel. The way They get Us to hate on each other. The Sacrifices, The Hopes and The Dreams. The Anger, The Despair, the need to jump ship instead of living Enslaved, The Wrongs. The Rage. And The Joy despite The Rage. And The Shame, all The Shame. I'm feeling it all, you know?

MISHA. You're high.

LEO. Yeah, I am. But I am also feeling the Feelings.

MISHA. This is big, L-train.

LEO. Wow. 'L-Train .' I still get, like a butterfly in my stomach when you call me that.

They kiss. MISHA *pulls away.*

We're both having an Experience.

MISHA. Technically, I'm still with Ralph.

LEO. Think of this as a revolutionary act.

MISHA. Brother, don't make the sister a tool in your revolution.

LEO *leans away. More smoking.*

LEO. His new friends. They're guys. White guys.
(*Rest.*)
He had already told them that I was his property. But I didn't know until I was standing in the middle of their circle. They wanted to know what it was like. Being a slave. I didn't say shit. That didn't go over too good. And I tried to leave but they weren't having that. They blocked the door. Ralph was like, play along with it. And – . And – . I tried to leave but. Then they started – uh, – bidding on me – . Throwing money on the floor. They surrounded me. I saw in my head all those horrible things that could happen to a brother or a sister in a situation like that. And I was so mad at myself for thinking that I was looking for an answer and I'd just ended up in more danger. That Ralph had put me in harm's way. All of a sudden I felt really ashamed. I don't know why but I did. Ashamed of what? I dunno. Some of the guys looked familiar. I felt like I'd seen some of them around. I don't know where but they looked like, people I might know, maybe. They looked like – just people. And I thought, it won't take much for one of them to cross the line and do whatever to me. Ralph, he should have been protecting me. That's what we agreed on. But what did I expect, right? I have been socially and genetically engineered to trust the Man. Free Will, the liberated operation of my own mind is not possible under these circumstances. And, and, all the while they were taunting me and saying shit, Ralph wasn't nowhere to be seen. I knew he was there, I knew he was there somewhere, but I couldn't see his face it. It was like – I couldn't tell him apart from the others.
(*Rest.*)

MISHA. It's time to quit.

LEO. I am 5 days away from discovering something through my own actual experience.

MISHA. All you have to do is walk away.

LEO. What if, one day, there's no longer a need for 'Ask A Black.' Cause, what if, one day, we overcome all of our stupid and divisive shit?

MISHA. There will always be stupid and divisive shit.

LEO. Sounds like you're banking on it.

MISHA. If we don't bank on it, then who will? They will. They already do.

LEO. Your Show is just as fucked up as my Quest. You want me to Quit. Why don't you Quit? Quit your Show. Quit Ralph. Just walk away.

MISHA. Maybe I love him.

LEO. Look who's got slave mentality.

She digs in her bag, taking out a magazine.

MISHA. Ralph got published.

LEO. Yeah, he said. Bragging about it. Waving the magazine around. He wrote about me being a slave, right?

MISHA. You read it yet?

LEO. Nope. You read it though, right?

MISHA. Not yet.
(*Rest.*)
Scared.

LEO. Read it to me.

They sit together. MISHA *prepares to read the article aloud to* LEO *as the lights fade.*

[*SLAVE-LABOR INTERLUDE: The days pass. The scenery changes.*]

Scene Eight: Ralph's Solo (Day 39)

RALPH. The Myth of the American Dream, the one that says that I was born to be on top of the world, that thing has got me hooked. Hook, line and sinker. I was a fucking fish. And I was drowning cause I was being reeled into a boat cause I had fallen for all the lines. Because the Myth said that I was a winner and I was sitting around wondering when I would get my Prize and the Prize wasn't coming. But now things are better.

(*Rest.*)

The <u>first</u> time I went to a Club meeting, it was trippy. I walked in and they were standing in a circle. I joined them. And then they did the opening – prayer. And the guys started talking, taking turns, real personal stuff. And me, I made a beeline for the door. And I stood there, not touching the doorknob but almost, and I thought, what the fuck, Ralph, this is your life. And you're a writer so this is material. And so, instead of walking out, I pretended like I was thirsty and I headed for the bar, actually just a table with a selection of drinks, and then, after a beer, I rejoined the circle. I was new, so they wanted me to share. I was just like blah blah blah blah blah. They sympathized with me about not getting the job. And – I'll admit it – that felt good.

(*Rest.*)

The Club meets every day of the week all around the city in different locations. All of them pretty upscale. It started out as mostly guys who needed a safe space where they could share openly and honestly. And over time, I guess, it grew into what it is. For me, after a couple of weeks, I started feeling grateful for the fellowship and, yeah, I wanted to impress them. The Dean was egging me on to spill it. So I mentioned the Leo thing. And the looks on their faces. And suddenly, I felt like somebody, like somebody who was doing something. Which is a new feeling for me.

(*Rest.*)

The guys at the Club. They affirm my feelings. It feels good to say things and not get judged. Everybody needs that, right? I started talking about my hopes and dreams. It was

embarrassing. Until they told me to stop sweating. That the world is my oyster, so shuck it.
(*Rest.*)
They took me shopping. Got me to spend my dad's money. Well, my money on myself. There's less hate in them than you would think. They talk about how they're losing their sense of place and me too, we are – we all are, feeling displaced. We talk about how we don't want to be passed over or excluded or disenfranchised. We want our piece of the pie. I mean, say you were sitting down at say, a Big Family Dinner and all the pie had been sliced and distributed and then someone comes in, late, some Johnny- or Janey-Come-Lately and you have to cut off a piece of your own pie so they could have some. Sure you'd do it but you'd feel sore, right? That's just what we're feeling. Sore. We're just a little sore. It's kind of a big sore, actually. Festering. There's a lot of anger. Hanging out with them, week after week, I can finally – relax into my own skin. And they're going to finance me, help me open up a chain of shooting ranges. They've got my back. So that's something, right?
(*Rest.*)
I told them about Leo, and yeah, they wanted to meet him. Up until then me and the Dean had kept it hush-hush. But you know how I am. People Pleaser. And Leo was cool with it, pretty much, so I brought him by. They asked Leo to stand in the middle of the circle. Just stand there. He did it. The guys, they couldn't believe it. They were amazed that he had agreed to the slave-thing. They asked him lots of questions, but Leo didn't feel like sharing the specifics; he totally closed up, he didn't want to talk about, you know, the why and the whatnot. So the guys all started looking at me, but I couldn't get him to talk. So, just making conversation, I asked them how much they thought he was worth. They gave some lowball numbers. And then Leo started talking about shooting and telling them what a great shot he is. And the guys, you know, cause it's <u>sports</u>, they totally believed him. They totally believed him so they placed their bets, wagering that Leo could, at the end of the 40-days, hit ten bullseyes in a row. And Leo, he was like, bring it on.

ACT TWO, SCENE EIGHT 109

And the guys were all so excited about him shooting
a perfect score and, if it was going to happen, they
wanted proof.
I could invite them all down to the Spot, but that would most
certainly get out of hand. So we're standing there with Leo in
the center, and one guy starts riffing. He had that auctioneer
thing down. And people started throwing money on the floor
at Leo's feet. Betting he'd win, betting he'd win. Leo was just
standing in the money. Not knowing what to do. And after a
while the evening was over and we all went home.
(*Rest.*)
Leo's Experiment, it wasn't my idea, and now we're telling
the world. I told The Club. He went on Misha's Show. And
now my phone is ringing off the hook. I've got offers to
appear, with Leo, in all the major markets. I got an agent.
We're talking endorsements, reality shows, fictional
adaptations. They want to know who I would like to play me
in the movie version of this. It's going to be great for both of
us. We're both going to cash in. Today is day 39. One more
day to go. Then we meet up at the Spot and party. Just the
four of us. At least that's the plan.
(*Rest.*)
Leo, he's totally wanting to do the wager. He totally wants to
show them his marksmanship. Only, I haven't seen him, Leo,
for like 5 days. Where is he? Nobody knows. I'm kind of
worried about him. I hope he's ok.
(*Rest.*)
I was waiting for the Prize to come but I am the Prize.
Nobody's talking about bringing back slavery, but I have been
feeling some real feelings and I've been mining the gold. And,
if Leo would just come back home, then we could take this
show on the road. Five days he's been gone. And I asked my
agents, if Leo continues his AWOL thing will the markets lose
interest and they are like, there is not a shelf life on this
material, man. This slave shit don't have an expiration date.
This is an endless goldmine. And I've struck it. Bullseye.

[SLAVE-LABOR INTERLUDE: The days pass. The scenery changes.]

Scene Nine: At the Spot (Day 40)

Night. The renovation is complete and the space has been decorated for a party. There's a banner that reads 'GRAND RE-OPENING!' There's a cake. There's drinks in an ice bucket. Only RALPH, MISHA *and* DAWN *are there.* LEO *is still AWOL.*

When they shoot they practice safety protocols. Wearing eyes and ears, only aiming down-range, etc. RALPH *shoots. He's pleased. He lays his gun back safely on the table.*

MISHA *shoots. She's more pleased. She lays her gun back safely on the table.* DAWN's *reading* RALPH's *story in the magazine.*

RALPH. I'm having the grand re-opening tomorrow night, but the banner works for our party too, right? The cake is chocolate on the inside. And I got chocolate icing even though the red white and blue writing would have shown up better on vanilla. When I told the cake lady that I wanted the cake to say 'FREEDOM' she asked me if my dad was getting out of prison.
(*Rest.*)
I think the cake is a nice touch.

DAWN. You're in The New Yorker, Ralph. Dream come fucking true.

RALPH. Leo's late.

MISHA. He's on 'Colored People's Time.'

RALPH. He's never late.

MISHA. Except that you haven't seen him in like a whole five days.

RALPH. Right.

MISHA. Your turn.

RALPH. Take it.

MISHA *shoots. She's pleased. She lays her gun back safely on the table.*

Did you see how I had the check printed out really big on that poster? 89 grand payable to Leo.

MISHA. It's a little tacky.

RALPH. I'm trying to make it festive.

MISHA. And the 40s, the malt liquor. Nice touch.

RALPH. Coming from you it means a lot.

RALPH *takes his shot. Not so pleased. He lays his gun back safely on the table.*

DAWN (*reading*). 'And what I learned from Miss Malvina is that waking up is hard to do but staying woke is harder.' The End.

RALPH. What do you think?

DAWN. 'Waking up is hard to do'?

RALPH. It sums it all up, right?

MISHA. The whole story, about the kid and Miss Malvina in the church basement and everything, that's Leo's story.

DAWN. Yeah, I was going to say that. Yeah.

RALPH. And Leo signed a contract saying that for 40 Days, he and everything of his would be my property. This was published during said 40 Days. So what's the problem?

MISHA. You're the problem.

DAWN. I liked it better when Leo told it. Just saying.

RALPH. He told it to us so many times. It became an old folk tale. I took it –

MISHA. You stole it.

RALPH. He wasn't doing anything with it. And I made it better.

MISHA. You're full of shit.

DAWN. And yet again, we've proven that nothing good ever comes out of slavery. Right?

> RALPH *shoots. He returns his gun to the table. He waits for the women to take their turns. They don't. He shoots again. And again.*

We should file a missing person's report.

MISHA. Leo ran <u>away</u>. He's a runaway slave.

DAWN. Where is he, you think?

MISHA. I am not my brother's keeper.

RALPH. If he doesn't show, we'll think of something.

MISHA. Maybe your white friends can help us find him.

DAWN. You went back to that Club?

RALPH. One more reason to hate on Ralph.
(*Rest.*)
Me and Leo are going to cash in big time on this. It's nothing like it was historically, not brutal like back in the day, but that's exactly what makes it interesting. Cause it shows how all the institutionalized microaggressions are still here, yeah, they're mirrored in every single relationship that exists today.

MISHA. And let me guess: You'll both cash in but you'll get the lion's share.

RALPH. The packaging is all my idea, so, yeah.

> RALPH *shoots again.*

DAWN. You think he's ok with you stealing his story?

RALPH. He'll profit from all this. I'll profit from all this. 'Ask A Black' is turning profit too.

MISHA. That's different. I actually have skin in the game. This skin. This Black skin. I'm making bank on something that's mine.

ACT TWO, SCENE NINE   113

RALPH. The whole thing. It belongs to everybody.

DAWN. Not in the same way.

RALPH. We disagree.

MISHA. Who are you even?

RALPH. I am who I've always been.

MISHA. And we are just here for Leo. Just so you know.

For something to do, MISHA *shoots.* DAWN *looks over the guns but doesn't choose one.*

RALPH. You're really going to take that new job?

DAWN. Upside is: I'll be working in community with a lot of people in need. Making sure they're not, you know, forgotten. I'll be making a difference.

MISHA. Sounds great. Good for you.

DAWN. Downside is: I'll have to relocate. But it's a great opportunity. It's a top-notch firm so it's worth it. You think Leo will wanna move?

MISHA. Ask him.

DAWN *shoots.*

RALPH. You hit the paper. Good job. You need help packing up your place?

DAWN. No, Ralph, I got it.

RALPH. Maybe one day I could be on one of those Do-Gooder committees you're always trying to get me to join.

DAWN. Thanks, but, I don't – I think – . No thanks, Ralph.

RALPH. Ok.

Passing the time. RALPH *shoots.* MISHA *shoots.* DAWN *shoots.*

DAWN. It's a great job. A really righteous opportunity.

MISHA. Yeah, you'll keep saving people and you'll also keep getting your ego boost. Win win.

DAWN. At the core of everybody who does good, is something that's less than good. That's always been true. In me, in you, in everybody.

MISHA. Don't lump me in with your apology.

DAWN. Your show cashed in on Leo. You let him embarrass himself. Then you invited in a string of guests to talk about him like he was some freak in a freak show. And now your show's a hit. Good for you.

MISHA. Don't patronize me.

RALPH. Ladies, play nice.

MISHA. Ralph, guess what? You and me? We're done.

RALPH. Well, whatever. Cause these past 40 days, I mean, full disclosure, I've been feeling very free.

RALPH *gestures suggestively toward* DAWN *providing* MISHA *with an understanding.*

MISHA. Fuck you.

MISHA *lunges at* RALPH *but he stops her.*

RALPH. Don't cry, Meesh.

MISHA. I'll cry if I fucking want to.

She sees that DAWN *is watching, listening.*

You're just loving this aren't you?

DAWN. No. Not at all.

LEO *has entered.*

MISHA. Hey, L-train.

LEO. Hey.

DAWN. You're good?

LEO. I'm here.

RALPH. You made it before midnight. 10 minutes to go. You're like Cinderella.

LEO. If you say so. Mr Ralph.

ACT TWO, SCENE NINE 115

RALPH. Where the hell have you been for the last five days?

LEO. None of your fucking business.

LEO
RALPH

MISHA. L-Train, you good?

LEO. I'm great. How's your Show?

MISHA. Sky's the limit.

> DAWN *gives* LEO *a hug*.

DAWN. Good to see you. Right? Hey, I've been thinking. We could, maybe, you know, try –

LEO. Dawn. I returned the ring, FYI. Ok?

DAWN. Oh. Ok.

LEO. And I heard you got a new job. Good luck to you. Really. All the best.

DAWN. Thanks. I want to make sure you're ok.

LEO. I'm ok. I'm great. I'll see you around.

DAWN. Right.
   (Rest.)
   We used to all be friends.

MISHA. Yeah. But now we're for real.

DAWN
LEO
MISHA
RALPH

RALPH. Let's keep in touch.

DAWN
DAWN
DAWN
(Rest.)

> DAWN *leaves*.

116   WHITE NOISE

MISHA. Come on, man, let's go.

LEO. I'm all right.

MISHA. You don't got to stay.

LEO. I do. I just got here. I gotta finish what I started.

MISHA. Let's go.

LEO. Let the brother cross the finish line, ok?

MISHA
MISHA
MISHA
(*Rest*.)

> MISHA *wipes her eyes, and wipes her hands of it. She goes.*

RALPH. Women. Right?

> RALPH *goes to the tub of drinks. Selects one. Downs it.*
>
> *Then he activates the target-retrieval system. The paper target that they were using earlier comes back. He refreshes it with a crisp paper bullseye-style target. Sends the target back.*

You like the decor?

LEO. You spared no expense.
(*Rest*.)
Is the wager-thing still happening?

RALPH. Yeah and quite a few are betting that my Leo will shoot 10 bullseyes in a row.

LEO. What about you? You in my corner?

RALPH. I am not. This was going to be a party, cause I was thinking we could win together right, but, reading the room, now I'm thinking: You are going to stumble and I am going to cash in.

LEO. You're an asshole.

RALPH. Don't hate the player, hate the game. Pick your pistol.

RALPH *gestures toward the table. Unloaded pistols and magazines of ammo. As* LEO *chooses his pistol,* RALPH *takes his father's pistol out of the carrying case, loads the magazine.*

Usually Masters don't let their slaves handle guns, but I got my special protection.

LEO. I read your story.

RALPH. Yeah. And time's a-wasting! Let's see you shoot. 10 in a row! Now.

LEO *puts on his eyes and ears. And a shooting glove. Prepares himself.*

I'm going to video this.

LEO. /Whatever/

RALPH. /The guys are sticklers for proof. Especially when there's money on the line/

LEO. /I said whatever.

RALPH*'s got the phone-video set up.*

RALPH (*into his phone*). Can Leo Hit It And Quit It?

LEO *shoots. Bullseye.*

LEO. Yes.

RALPH. Right in the center! One down, nine to go.

LEO *relaxes his stance.*

RALPH *gets another beer. Downs it.*

And you gotta use a different gun each time.

LEO. Those aren't the rules.

RALPH. They are now. And each gun is only loaded with a single bullet, so you <u>have</u> to change, else you'll be just be shooting blanks. Fun right?

LEO goes to the table, unloading his gun and choosing another one. Loading up.

Want some cake?

LEO. No thanks.

RALPH. Right. The sugar might throw you.

LEO puts down his gun, goes over to the cake. Looks at it.

It says 'Freedom.'

LEO. I can see that.

LEO cuts himself a big slice. Eats. Wipes his hands on his pants. Takes up his gun. Shoots. Another bullseye.

RALPH. Bullseye number two! Good for you! Two's company three's a crowd. But you want a crowd tonight, don't you?

LEO fires the gun repeatedly in the air. Its magazine is empty so we just hear the clicks.

Each pistol only gets one bullet. I can't have you picking your favorite gun and getting all comfortable with it.

Abiding by the new 'rules,' LEO chooses another pistol. Another magazine of ammo.

You wanna get three in a row. I feel you. Funny what they call a 'threesome' these days, right? A 'Thrupple.' Crazy world we live in, right? Agree with me.

LEO. I agree with you.

LEO has chosen and loaded his new pistol. He concentrates his energy. Shoots. Another bullseye.

RALPH. Three in a row! A Thrupple! Three strikes! You're out! Just kidding! Good job, but just so we all know, three is a long way from a perfect ten. I have never dated a '3.'

LEO chooses a fresh pistol loads it.

I feel like I'm a solid 7. I used to see myself as a 5. But I was lowballing, right? I'm a seven. And I've never dated below 5.

ACT TWO, SCENE NINE   119

Dawn and Misha both are 8-9s and when they clean up they could each pass for 10s depending on the cultural context.
(*Rest.*)
Did you like going to the Club? Meeting the guys?

LEO. You lied to me about who they were. What it was. You said they were Art Gallery people.

RALPH. Some of them were. Most of them were not. But they were all really impressed with you. Bragging about your marksmanship. You were a hit. You were Mr Hot Shot. And they all want so much to be great at something.

LEO. I wouldn't have gone there if I had known.

RALPH. Exactly.

LEO readies himself. Concentrating his energy. LEO *shoots. Another bullseye.*

Hambone! Four in a row. Six more to go. Will he make it? I dunno! <u>Oh No</u>! He's a Ho!

LEO. What?!

RALPH. Just rhyming. 'You worry yourself unnecessarily. Put the thought of hitting the target right out of your mind!'

LEO. You're quoting 'Zen in the Art of Archery.' The guy who wrote it was basically a Nazi.

RALPH. One man's trash is another man's treasure.

RALPH *gets another beer.*

Instead of choosing a pistol off the table, LEO *picks up* RALPH's *gun. Heads into position.*

He's using his Master's weapon. Can't say I like that, but as he's already in position –

LEO *shoots. Another bullseye.*

Five golden bulls! Good for you.

LEO <u>unloads</u> RALPH's gun *and puts it safely back from where it came from.*

He removes his eyes and ears and goes to the tub of beers, fishing through them, checking out the different brands.

RALPH *takes a quick look over his gun. Puts the magazine back in, reloading it. Places it safely down.*

LEO *opens a bottle of beer. Downs it. Then he selects another pistol. Loads it. Replaces his eyes and ears. Stands in position and, with some swagger this time, shoots. Another perfect shot.*

Six-pack. 6 in a row. 4 more to go.

LEO. You don't like me touching your piece?

RALPH. Correct. I don't like you touching my piece. Yeah.

LEO. It was my story. And you went and stole it.

RALPH. Under the terms of the contract –

LEO. You stole it and you had it published under your name.

LEO *chooses a new pistol. Prepares.*

RALPH. It's not like you were trying to get it published. I took it and made it into something beautiful. The only time you ever told it was to get pity from whoever would listen.

LEO. You stole my story and you turned all the people into white people.

RALPH. I made it more relatable.

LEO. And you called the story 'Woke.'

RALPH. It's a great title.

LEO. Fuck you.

LEO *shoots. Another bullseye.* RALPH *gets another beer.*

RALPH. Everything's just a bunch of Stories. Just a bunch of stories. Sometimes they're yours sometimes they're somebody else's. Everybody's got a right to everything. Get over it.

(Into his phone.)

7 in a row for the folks at home. Folks at home might be thinking right now that Leo here, such a fine specimen. So well-trained. Folks at home, you all might be thinking that Leo, King of the Range, can make another three bullseyes no sweat! Bet high and win big, guys.

LEO *has chosen and loaded a fresh pistol.*

RALPH *fiddles with his phone, adjusting the angle.*

We're about to take shot number –

Cutting RALPH *off mid-sentence,* LEO *shoots. Another bullseye.*

– That was bullseye number 8. If there had been 8 wildebeast crossing the savannah you would have bagged all 8 of them. An 8-bagger. 8 in a row!

LEO *looks into the phone.*

LEO. Fuck all you all.

RALPH. Anger was never good for your concentration. Are you angry?

LEO *returns his pistol.*

Get angry if you want but you don't want to make them mad.

LEO. I'm not angry.

RALPH. I gave Dawn a lesson.

LEO. Yeah. Ok. So.

RALPH. Did you think she was the one?

LEO. What's it to you?

RALPH. We hooked up. A week or so ago. I didn't force her. It was pretty much a mutual thing. You two wouldn't have lasted anyway. She's pretty desperate for a winner.

LEO *chooses another pistol. Loads it. Then he looks into the phone again.*

LEO. Fuck all you all. Every single one. You heard me.

LEO *shoots. Another bullseye.*

RALPH. Another bullseye. If we were bowling it'd be called 'A Golden Turkey.' 9 in a row. Almost but not quite there. Good job seeing as how you're out of practice.

LEO *is choosing another gun.*

LEO. Oh, I've been practicing.

RALPH. Where?

LEO. In my head.

LEO
RALPH

RALPH. What's 40 minus 5?

LEO. What's your point?

RALPH. You owe me 5 more days. The agreement said 40 and you ran away with 5 days to go.

LEO. Let's call it even.

RALPH. Let's not. You owe me. Five. Days. You owe me 5 days or I'm not legally obligated to pay you.

LEO. That money is nothing to you.

RALPH. But it's everything to you.
(*Rest.*)
Ok. Here's the deal. Make 10 in a row you get your money and your five days. Fuck up lose the money and you spend five more days with me.

LEO. Deal. Fine.

RALPH. Ok. Only one more to go. One away from perfection. Not that you'll make it. Or maybe you will. One more shot. Make it or break it. Shit gentlemen, maybe you'll win, cause this Leo, this Leo right here, he can shoot a perfect ten in his sleep.

LEO. Except that I haven't been sleeping. For the past 5 days. I've been walking around the city, wide awake again.

RALPH. You seem on-edge.

LEO. I'm fine. Sheer force of will.

RALPH. Glad to hear it. What about that hissing?

LEO. The hissing sound never left.

RALPH. Is it comforting? That sound?

LEO. No.

RALPH. Sorry to hear that.
   (*Rest.*)
   Take your shot. One more. Come on.

LEO *is facing down-range.*

LEO. I've been walking around town and I've been thinking. I'm thinking so hard. I'm trying so hard. Trying to see a way. – . I mean, who were they exactly, my ancestors? I don't even know all their names. I bought into the shame. Cause erasing my past is part of the plan. If you erase my past you can erase my future. *Ssssss*. I get it.

RALPH. I hope you don't miss.

LEO. I got the rage. I also got the Higher Power. Horrible shit went down back in the day and horrible shit goes down every day but, if it ain't never going away, then that'll just be how it is. And my people, my people who came before me, what they lived through, and what they fought and died for, all that is more than plenty to help me make it through any kind of day in any kind of way. And I love them, because they made it. And I love them, so I can make it. I am the Evidence. And no thing, no body, no system, no way, no how can make me forget myself.

RALPH. Maybe you're going to miss. Maybe you won't even hit the paper. That could happen. Even to you.

LEO. I'm done playing.

RALPH. Dig down deep. What do you hear?

LEO. There's that hissing. That hissing sound.

RALPH. Yeah.
  (*Rest.*)
  Sssss. It will always be the loudest thing you hear. You got it in your head and it'll stay there forever. And I put it there. Maybe I've had you trained from way back. Cause that's how this world works, Bro.

LEO *puts the gun to his own head.*

LEO
LEO
LEO

Then he points the gun to the ceiling. And fires. The gun shoots into the ceiling. LEO *fires repeatedly but after the initial shot we only hear empty clicks.*

LEO *drops the gun on the ground. He's exhausted. Spent.*

RALPH. Oh, that's a shame. So close and yet so far.

RALPH *turns off the camera. Puts his own gun away. Wrapping things up.*

That means we've got another 5 days to go. But it's not so bad, is it? What you went through?

LEO *shoves* RALPH *aside and gets ahold of* RALPH*'s gun. And then he turns the gun on* RALPH. LEO *has* RALPH *in his sights.*

Large and in charge now, huh? Not that you'd know how to run shit even if you got the chance, but who cares! Here comes the revolution! Kill me. Go ahead and kill me. I know you want to. I know you want to!

LEO *could kill* RALPH. *They face each other.*

LEO
RALPH
LEO
RALPH
LEO
RALPH

LEO *lifts his gaze, toward the ancestors.*

LEO. I'm awake! I'M AWAKE!

LEO *ejects the magazine, which clatters to the floor.* LEO *keeps ahold of the empty gun.*

And, as LEO *watches,* RALPH *crumbles to the floor and sobs.*

The End.

*<u>ADDENDUM</u>

AMENDMENTS

Amendment #1: During the 40-day period, and after the successful completion of said 40 days, both parties agree to non-disclosure in all media.

Amendment #2: During the 40-day period, The Enslaved Person agrees to neither read nor write.

Amendment #3: During the 40-day period, The Enslaved Person agrees to relinquish the possession and the use of his phone.

Amendment #4: During the 40-day period, The Enslaved Person agrees to allow the Master Person to physically discipline him when the situation warrants it. What warrants the punishment is the decision of the Master and the means of the punishment are also the Master's decision.

Amendment #5: During the 40-day period, The Enslaved Person agrees to accept physical advances of the Master in the unlikely event that the Master desires him.

Amendment #6: During the 40-day period, The Enslaved Person agrees that his person might be transferrable, that is, that the Master could share The Enslaved Person with whomever The Master deems appropriate and that the Enslaved Person will not receive additional financial compensation for this additional labor.

SIGNED AND AGREED TO BY

Master

Enslaved Person

Date

www.nickhernbooks.co.uk

facebook.com/nickhernbooks
twitter.com/nickhernbooks